THE RUNNER

Also by David Samuels

Only Love Can Break Your Heart

The Runner

A True Account of the Amazing Lies and
Fantastical Adventures of the
Ivy League Impostor James Hogue

DAVID SAMUELS

THE NEW PRESS

NEW YORK
LONDON

Author's Note: Portions of this book appeared in sketchier form in my article about James Hogue's time at Princeton, which appeared in the September 3, 2001, issue of *The New Yorker*. That article was also titled "The Runner."

I would like to thank Keith Mark, Jon Luff, Brian Sax, Brian Patrick, Cindy Putnam, Dr. Louis Alaia, SuperStar, Detective Robert Walraven, the Mountain Village police department, and the many other people who took the time to speak with me about James Hogue during the years it took me to research and write this book.

I would also like to thank Maury Botton, Sarah Fan, Henry Finder, Miriam Gross, Virginia Heffernan, Ben Metcalf, Jesse Moss, Zoe Pagnamenta, Andrew Wylie, and Dr. J. Gerald Young for their help in bringing this story to print.

Requests for permission to reproduce selections from this book should be mailed to:
Permissions Department, The New Press, 38 Greene Street, New York, NY 10013.

Published in the United States by The New Press, New York, 2008
Distributed by W. W. Norton & Company, Inc., New York

LIBRARY OF CONGRESS CATALOGING-IN-PUBLICATION DATA

Samuels, David, 1967 Mar. 3–
The runner : a true account of the amazing lies and fantastical adventures
of the Ivy League impostor James Hogue / David Samuels.
    p.   cm.
ISBN 978-1-59558-188-4 (hc.)
1. Hogue, James Arthur, 1959–   2. Imposters and imposture—Colorado—
Telluride—Biography.   3. Runners (Sports)—Colorado—Telluride—Biography.
4. Telluride (Colo.)—Biography.   5. Princeton University—Biography.   I. Title.
CT9981.H64S26   2008
364.16'3092—dc22
[B]   2007035004

The New Press was established in 1990 as a not-for-profit alternative to the large,
commercial publishing houses currently dominating the book publishing industry.
The New Press operates in the public interest rather than for private gain, and is
committed to publishing, in innovative ways, works of educational, cultural, and
community value that are often deemed insufficiently profitable.

www.thenewpress.com

A Caravan Book
For more information, visit www.caravanbooks.org

Composition by dix!

Printed in the United States of America

2   4   6   8   10   9   7   5   3   1

For Virginia

Ad astra per aspera

—Official motto, State of Kansas

THE RUNNER

Telluride

I. The Stranger

Early in the morning of January 9, 2006, a slight, boyish-looking man walked down a snow-covered dirt road outside Telluride, Colorado, with the aim of leaving his old life behind him. Wearing a hooded sweatshirt to hide his face, he carried a pack on his back and a single duffle bag by his side, having dumped most of his worldly possessions near a water tower in a nearby forest.

Though he lived frugally and enjoyed a mostly solitary existence, the fugitive had also made a surprising number of friends in Telluride, a wealthy ski town whose population is more or less evenly split among rich vacationers and landowners, the craftsmen who build and repair their houses, and immigrants from Mexico and Eastern Europe who do menial jobs. Some knew him as a world-class distance runner who had competed at the highest levels of his sport and who still ran twenty miles a day in the winter on the mountain trails. Others believed that he was an Ivy League–educated engineer who had moved to Telluride six years earlier to build houses. His close friends believed the same story that he was a master carpenter who had spent time in Italy. Visitors to Telluride knew him as a successful entrepreneur who traveled the world installing custom-built safes in private homes. He dated beautiful women, and could converse in Swedish, Norwegian, and the Swiss-German dialect. He spoke fluent Italian as well as Russian, which he used to communicate with his girlfriend, a gorgeous blonde doctor who was preparing to join him in town. An expert downhill skier who had appeared as a stunt double in ski movies, he was also a capable cook who baked his own bread and prided himself on his knowledge of food and wine.

The fact that no two stories about the stranger were the same could be explained by his preference for letting other people do the talking. Even his close friends had a hard time remembering exactly where his stories left off and their own imaginations took over, and so the most basic facts about his life remained in dispute long after he skipped town. He was from Wyoming or else he was from Kansas. He graduated from the University of Texas, the University of Wyoming, Stanford University, and Princeton University, with graduate degrees in biomedical engineering, chemistry, mechanical engineering, or geology. While none of the stories that were told about him were literally true, all of them bore some degree of family resemblance to the actual story of a life that would leave nearly everyone in town scratching their heads and wondering how and why they had been fooled.

Departing in haste on a cold winter morning, the young-looking man, who pretended to be in his late twenties (he was forty-seven years old when he vanished from Telluride) left behind a collection of over seven thousand objects secreted in a hidden room in his basement, in and around his small house, and in a rented storage locker several miles away. Each of these trophies testified to his success in constructing a series of fictional identities for himself while penetrating deeply into the lives of other people who had what he lacked—a stable sense of connection to his self, to his past, and to other people. Accounting for more than half the property crimes in Telluride over the better part of a decade, the collection was also a source of gifts that had helped the stranger make friends in town.

Depicted in hundreds of evidentiary photographs taken by the police after his departure, the stranger's hoard was a comical mix of expensive furnishings and junk. Among the stolen objects he left behind were a pair of moose antlers, a set of medical books, several stuffed bears, expensive racing bicycles, a trove of rare Honduran mahogany, over a dozen fine rugs valued at over $25,000, power tools, nineteenth-century landscape paintings and engravings of birds, a carousel horse, an antique rifle, a working modern rifle, a Weber grill, two sinks, fifteen black trash bags filled with expensive linens, a set of carefully polished copper cooking pans, and a large Princeton University decal suitable for application to the rear windshield of a car. In his refrigerator was a case of chilled Dom Pérignon champagne that he had stolen from his friend David Eckley, a local developer. "He was a sweetheart, but dangerous in his own way," Eckley told the *Denver Post*. "He just can't seem to come to reality."

While the value of the goods he stole in Telluride amounted to well over $100,000, his career as a thief was only part of his story, which was darker and more heartbreaking than anything that his friends, many of whom were also his victims, could have imagined. By the time the police obtained a new warrant for his arrest on January 10, 2006, the stranger had vanished from the state of Colorado. Based on the evidence he left behind, the police concluded that he intended to make a new life for himself in Russia, where his girlfriend lived. They believed that he might be intending to use his medical knowledge to pass himself off as a doctor, or to obtain medical training under a new name and then return to the United States.

Further research into the stranger's background revealed that some of the most remarkable details of his story were in fact true. The man who lived in a ramshackle cabin in the woods had indeed attended Princeton University, where his talents were so obvious, and his life story so captivating and unusual, that his classmates talked about him as a likely Rhodes Scholar. Instead, he became a kind of self-created mythic character whose memory lived on at Princeton, in Telluride, and the various other stops on his lonely and secretive journey. Driven by a compelling private logic, he had traveled from the desert to the mountains, from Texas, to California, to Utah, to Princeton, to Telluride, and places in between, while picking up and discarding a half dozen different identities. Along the way, he was convicted of nearly a dozen crimes, including three felonies. In his own mind, he was more like Bobby Fischer, playing a real-life version of chess against the institutions and laws that govern the actions of the solid majority. He took only what he felt he had to take. He was not violent. He only fooled people who wanted to be fooled.

At an altitude of almost nine thousand feet, surrounded by fourteen-thousand-foot-high mountain peaks, Telluride is a good place to come if you want to shed your skin and become someone new. The skiing is fantastic, with bright sunlight bouncing off dazzling white snow, so bright that it is impossible to ski the steep downhill runs without wearing dark goggles. The trails are shadowed by tall dark pines. The evenings in Telluride are like a photographic negative of the days, with ghostly, emptied-out mountains shadowing the velveteen darkness of the box canyon below. With a million stars in the sky visible to the naked eye at once, the natural beauty of Telluride at night can be overwhelming in a way that the surface dazzle of the snow on the slopes can't match.

Telluride is a place where time moves in a different way than it does on the coasts. History starts, and then it goes into hibernation, and then it starts over again, twenty or fifty years later. For a period of more than decade, much of the wealth of the Americas came out of the mines here and in surrounding towns like Ophir and Placerville, in the last great gold strike on the American continent. Butch Cassidy robbed his first bank in Telluride, and more than one prominent local family is reputed to have made its money by providing whores to miners. There are nice boutiques and expensive restaurants that serve celebrity guests like Oprah Winfrey and Tom Cruise. The local TV station, Plum TV, caters to visitors who spend their winters in Telluride and their summers on Martha's Vineyard, an exceptionally tiny but profitable demographic that has replaced gold mining and drug dealing as Telluride's leading source of wealth.[1] It is easy to lose yourself here.

Bundled up in my black parka, I drove through the mountains with Jeremy Thompson, who is part of the floating population of ski bums and trust-fund kids and seekers who make their way here, and stay for a while before they move on. Before he came to Telluride, he was a park ranger in Denali in Alaska, the wilderness park where a young adventurer named Chris McCandless starved to death in an abandoned bus in August 1992, a story that inspired Jon Krakauer's book *Into the Wild*. Jeremy read a paperback copy of *Into the Wild* in Alaska, and enjoyed it very much. "Me and a bunch of my friends hiked out there to see the bus," he answered, when I asked him what he makes of people who venture off the beaten path and go it alone in such a radical fashion. As a fellow wanderer, he has a great deal of sympathy for McCandless. "I don't think he was so wrong as a lot of people said," he suggested. "I think he was trapped there. He didn't realize when he went in that the river would rise and he wouldn't be able to get out."

We rode for a while in silence, as the sky darkened and the detail of the mountains faded into a phosphorescent sea of whiteness that rose above us like a cresting wave. There is nothing like these mountains back east. The extraordinary steepness of the mountains combined with sudden rises and drops in temperature helps explain the large number of deadly avalanches, Jeremy said. We talked for a while about roaming around the country

---

1. The arrival of the drug dealers came after a coterie of West Coast hippies took over the town from the unemployed miners who were busy drinking themselves to death in the local bars. The smarter hippies soon got tired of gazing at the mountains and signed on with some out-of-state ski moguls to build a resort. The drug of choice in Telluride in the seventies was the white powder memorialized in the eighties coke ballad "Smuggler's Blues" by ex-Eagle Glenn Frey: "They move it through Miami, sell it in L.A./They hide it up in Telluride, I mean it's here to stay."

without any firm destination in mind, and the benefits and the drawbacks of the traveling lifestyle. Eventually, the conversation circled back to McCandless.

"I could easily see myself doing the stuff that he did," Jeremy said. "I left home six years ago. I've been moving around ever since." McCandless was the victim of bad weather and bad information, Jeremy said. "One of his books, on edible plants, was incorrect. You try to prepare yourself, and then you have books that are misleading and there is no hospital next door."

Jeremy is an appealing kid, whose quiet, clueless manner, and his willingness to learn, reminds me of myself when I was his age. He grew up in Seattle and left home when he was eighteen, and traveled around Mexico and Latin America, making money and feeding his jones for travel. He headed up to Alaska, and made his way down to Colorado. The advantage of the traveling life is that you never get bored. For some people, it's the only thing they know. I told him about the years I spent wandering without a fixed address, and about the people that you meet riding buses in the Pacific Northwest.

In school, Jeremy was diagnosed with a speech impediment, which is just barely audible, a soft footfall hidden behind lace-curtain consonants. Because of his diagnosis, he explained, he was placed in special education classes, where he stayed until he left school. The kids in special classes aren't any dumber than anyone else, he said. It's just that the school district gets paid extra for each kid. "I needed to run away," he told me. He has six brothers and sisters. His father worked all the time. In the mountains it gets dark by five thirty. Stands of pale white aspen trees lined the snow-covered roads that took us even higher up into the mountains on our way out to Rico.

Sitting behind the wheel of his Jeep, in his parka and blue jeans, Jeremy was a dead ringer for James Hogue, the fugitive who was also known as Alexi Indris-Santana, Jay Mitchell Huntsman, and various other people with false names and invented histories who might be best understood as more or less temporary incarnations of a single transcendent spirit or idea. What Hogue's avatars had in common was that they led highly individual lives, ran long distances, alternately captivated and betrayed the people they met, and inevitably wound up in jail. Jeremy had heard about the drifter who stole from everyone in town, and who educated himself using only his wits and his talent for telling fantastical stories designed to ingratiate himself with the people he encountered along the way. "In an ideal world, he'd just be a hero, and he wouldn't steal," he said. "But if he saw what he needed to do, and he did it, what's so terrible about that?"

Having spent the past ten years tracking Hogue's strange journey across America, I was tempted to agree. Hogue's impostures showed no small amount of resourcefulness and courage, which are qualities that I admire. They also had the effect of showing up some of the larger deceptions and impostures that serve as the foundation of the American class system, which we sometimes celebrate and occasionally criticize as an affront to the Jeffersonian democratic ideal. Hogue also did what all liars do, which is to diminish the universal store of truthfulness that makes it possible for human beings to connect to something larger than themselves through language, which makes it possible for us to learn new things and establish meaningful connections to others.

Now both the trees and the snow had vanished into the darkness, and all that was visible along the road are the headlights of the occasional passing cars and the moonlight on the high mountain peaks. My feet were extra warm from the heater in the Jeep. Jeremy believes that a person can become whoever he wants. He wanted to go to college and study Spanish, he said, but it was too expensive, so he went to Mexico instead. I studied the ice patterns on the window as they are illuminated by the reflection of our high-beam lights off the snow-covered pines. It was easy to see why Jim chose to make Telluride his home. "You'll lack luxuries, such as comfort and companionship, and at other times (or at the same time) you'll even miss out on necessities, such as food, sleep and shelter," he wrote in a personal essay that defined his fervent approach to existence, submitted in his application to Princeton University. "You may be excited, bored, confused, desperate and amazed all in the same day. Or hour."

Telluride is one of the most beautiful places on earth, Jeremy agreed. But there is something about the town that bothers him. It's not so much the people who come here to ski, he said, but the people who own these huge houses and live in them for two weeks a year. While stealing is wrong, there is a part of him that hoped all along that James Hogue would make good on his promise and escape once more.

Cindy Putnam lives with her husband in a stand of new houses in a valley in Rico. There aren't enough new houses to call the place where Cindy lives a neighborhood, or a new development, or even a subdivision. It looks like ten or twelve families found some decent land in a good location at a reasonable price and decided to cash in their chips and settle here. During the day she cleans other people's houses, and she keeps her own small house impeccably clean and neat, without a single potted plant or remote control or paperback book out of place. She is a gorgeous older woman from Iowa with long blond hair that cascades down to the middle of her shoulder blades and the translucent skin of someone who has achieved a state of exceptional good health by paring away every stray gram of sugar and fat and every other substance that is not absolutely essential to proper nutrition. Her husband does landscaping, and their son Robin is in his second year of art school in Oregon. She was Hogue's friend and running partner here in Telluride, although she still hasn't visited him in jail.

Settling in on her beige couch with a glass of white wine, Cindy told me that she first met Hogue in January of 2000, on a bike path about three miles out of town. For a serious runner, not running, even in the dead of winter in the Colorado Rockies, isn't really an option, unless you take up skiing in a serious way. She is forty-eight years old, and started running in college in Montana. She ran nineteen miles a day with Hogue and her friend Kari Distefano, who ran for the U.S. team in the Olympics. She ran on the bike path because the trails were full of snow. One reason that she keeps running, she told me, is that she enjoys the runner's high, the feeling of losing track of time and being transported outside the limits of your own body. "I guess that it keeps me running," she said, smiling brightly, sitting up straight with her legs curled up beneath her.

There is something entirely innocent but also mischievous about Cindy, a kind of introvert's sense of humor that makes it very pleasant to talk with her. The runner's high is more like spacing out while driving at night than getting high on drugs, she explained. You can vanish entirely inside your own head.

"I just remember the day I met him," she said, of her sometime running companion. "He was running towards me, and there's probably thirty or forty people who run fairly regularly in Telluride. And I didn't recognize this guy."

It's easy for Telluride runners to spot tourists, even if they're in pretty good shape. World-class runners often choose to live or train in places like Boulder and Albuquerque in order to improve their ability to absorb oxygen. The towns they choose for training purposes tend to be about five thousand feet above sea level. Telluride is closer to nine thousand feet, and the lung-expanding benefits of breathing the oxygen-thin air are outweighed by a decrease in the rate of leg turnover, which makes high-altitude runners slower when they return to sea level. Cindy had reached the turnaround point on the bike path, a scenic pathway through the forests outside of Telluride, when Hogue stopped and stretched, and then began running towards her. "He had great form, and he was running towards me really fast," she remembered. "Usually I'm competitive enough that I'll try to not let somebody catch me," she added. She quickly realized that she didn't stand much of a chance of outrunning her new companion, who turned out to be modest and encouraging. "He said, 'Oh no, I'm just trying to get back into running. I haven't run much since college.' "

The man she met barely looked thirty, which meant that he was still at his peak as a distance runner. She introduced her new friend to Kari Distefano, who could run faster than any man in Telluride. Running up to twenty miles a day together, Cindy and Kari learned that their new friend had in fact been an Olympic-caliber runner, until he had suffered a trauma that had stopped his college running career cold. Arriving at the University of Wyoming on a track scholarship, he told them, he had found himself competing against more mature Kenyan athletes in their late twenties who had been recruited by the college and were headed for the Olympics.

"Kari got a big kick out of the story, 'cause she thinks that it's great for American distance running that the Kenyans did show up and forced everybody to run faster," Cindy remembered. "But I felt sort of bad for him." She was charmed by Hogue's offhand humor, and his modest, boy-next-door demeanor. When she complained about her worn-out gloves, he brought her a brand-new pair of expensive Marmot ski gloves that he claimed to have found at a swap meet.

Hogue also showed a parental interest in Cindy's son Robin, who was then twelve years old and having trouble in school. "He'd tell me, 'Well, you know, he draws all the time, and he writes,' " she remembered, trying out a dead-on imitation of Hogue's quiet drawl. " 'I wouldn't worry about him. He's obviously a smart kid.' "

In addition to his degree from the University of Wyoming, Cindy learned, Hogue had a master's degree in engineering from Princeton University. He had purchased a large ranch in the San Luis Valley, a remote and shockingly beautiful area with huge valleys shadowed by some of Colorado's tallest mountains. The nearest town was Cuchara, a small ski area that was famous for getting lots of natural snow, and for attracting a mixed bag of artists and writers and cultlike Christian groups who shared in common an attraction to extreme isolation and natural beauty.

There is an inspirational quote from the runner George Sheehan that Cindy had found in an old issue of *Runner's World* magazine and mentioned to me earlier in our conversation: "The more I run, the more I want to run, and the more I live a life conditioned and influenced and fashioned by my running." Running, she says, can give you a sense of purpose, and it can also drive you deeper into your own head. When she was younger, Cindy told me, and didn't have any money to travel, she used to enjoy making up stories about having lived in faraway places like New Zealand. She told these stories to people she met at bars or parties and whom she was unlikely to ever see again.

Cindy's habit of telling tall tales is familiar. On long bus trips, talking with strangers, I made up a past for myself as a kid who'd grown up on U.S. Army bases. I had never been to a U.S. Army base in my life, I told Cindy. Perhaps there was something I was trying to express about myself that could best be expressed in a lie. I'd moved around a lot in my twenties, and grew up outside of what might be generally considered to be normal American society. I was raised by a loving mother who worked and a loving father who was subject to sudden, intense outbursts of anger which in my adulthood I have mostly taken out on myself by smoking two or three packs of cigarettes a day and using illegal drugs. In a funny way, the drugs connected me to my childhood, because they gave me a solid feeling of connection to a higher truth that was invisible to everyone around me. I was raised in an orthodox Jewish community where I wore special clothes that were intended to set me apart from the people I saw on the street. I prayed three times a day, observing holidays and fast days where it was forbidden to drink a glass of water or swallow a mouthful of toothpaste. Partly as a result of my father's anger, or the suffocating austerity of the lifestyle that was imposed upon our family, or my own faulty chemistry—who knows why, exactly?—I felt uncomfortable in my own skin. I remember getting off the bus one day in my late twenties, and walking in the rain—I think I was going from Portland to Eugene, Oregon.

"That's where my son is in school," Cindy interrupted. It rains all the time in Eugene, I told her. The experience of walking away from that bus felt like the way Cindy described the runner's high. Where did those last five miles go? There was something scary about the ease with which I became a new person, a fictional character, with attributes that had bubbled to the surface five minutes ago and had never been part of my identity before. The person sitting next to me conducted a long conversation with a made-up person that wasn't me, while I sat somewhere off to the side, observing. The sense of power I obtained through the practice of self-abstraction was undeniable. At the same time I felt cold inside, and detached from my own body.

Perhaps one reason that James Hogue has held my interest for the past ten years is that I still can't figure out exactly what he was up to, at the same time as he reminded me strongly of myself. I felt like there was an understanding between us that would make it possible for us to speak with each other in a meaningful way. He was a member of the Ivy Club at Princeton. He was a homeless drifter who exposed the emptiness and pretense at the heart of the so-called American meritocracy. He was an impostor, a teller of fantastical tales, a perversely self-destructive imp. My Russian grandfather would have called Hogue a *chort*—a devil. I found him mildly amusing and mildly off-putting in person, but I took pleasure in the mischievous spirit that animated his cons. The best of his lies were only minor, handmade versions of the greater institutional lie that has encouraged any number of successful Ivy League graduates to believe that their youthful achievements were something other than an inheritance from their parents and grandparents. He was Exhibit A in my personal catalog of reasons why the Ivy League should be abolished, a cause to which he contributed in a unique and highly original way that all the self-satisfied inheritors of privilege around him could never have dreamed up, even as he hurt some of the people that he met in ways that they could never forgive or forget.

Hogue was a convicted fabulist who attempted again and again to impose the freaks of his imagination on the world around him, a practice that struck me as being entirely in the American vein. Americans are fibbers. Our national literature celebrates the whopper and the tall tale, beginning with the story of the boy who could not tell a lie. The fact that we lie like crazy while pretending to always tell the truth is such a common narrative strategy in American literature and American lives that we frequently confuse our wishful imaginings with reality. Living with one foot in the present and one foot in the future, we native optimists often feel that we have little choice but to make things up, a slippery procedure that can lead to the full-scale onset of the liar's disease from which I am in no way immune.

I, too, had lied about the year I was born. I met people on buses and I lied to them for hours, beginning with my name and where I was from, and continuing on to encompass every last detail of my present and past, in the hopes that my stories would help them feel comfortable enough to open up and tell me intimate details of their lives. The immediate effect of these lies was never less than exhilarating. The best comparison I can think of would be the rush of hot air into a hot air balloon as it wobbles and shakes until the ropes are released and it begins to rise into dreamless blue skies of the prime-time television commercials for the powerful drugs that regulate levels of serotonin in the brain.

The lies I told were products of circumstance, and of some real and obvious instability in my own character. They were born of a lifelong habit of listening and watching and pretending, through methods ranging from strategic silence to deliberate prevarication. I lied because I had to. I lied because I felt like it. When I met people from the South, I spoke to them in a gentle Southern accent. I wondered how many made-up versions of myself I would run through until I arrived at the me that felt right. Lying, by omission, and with the intent to deceive, is part of the equipment of my chosen profession. It is also a part of the price that a classless society demands of those who would dream of escaping the station into which they were born.

I stopped telling stories about my past because I felt like I might lose track of myself in some permanent way, I told Cindy. I felt like I might do serious damage to the feeling of being a whole, real person.

"Me too!" she said, happy to share her stories of youthful deception with another recovered liar. Maybe lying is a phase to which imaginative introverts who are particularly desperate to connect with reality are prone. I remembered that Jim's friend David Eckley said that part of him hoped that Jim would get away. I wondered what is so attractive about a grown-up person who can't stop lying.

"It's like somebody that's not real," Cindy said. "It's like something that maybe we all kind of want to be, or try on." Jim's goal was not to become rich, or to become better educated. Those goals were only secondary to his true purpose, which was spookier and more unsettling, and more universal. He turned his life into a story in order to escape from reality.

"It's why I love to read fiction," she said. To become a fictional character is a scary, high-altitude thought, she agreed, especially for people who spend a lot of time inside their own heads. It would take an incredible amount of dedication and endurance to pull off a stunt like that.

"I can't imagine how it would feel anything but lonely," she said. She and her husband moved to Telluride because it was the most beautiful place they had ever seen.

"I guess I'm just one of those shallow people that needs a really beautiful place to live," she said. The part of Iowa where she grew up was dead flat. "I am addicted to beauty," she sighed. "I can't help it. I could never live out on the plains."

II. An Extraordinary Young Man

Floating one thousand feet above Telluride is a snow-capped and pleasantly artificial version of an Alpine village done up in winterized hues of the tan and stucco palette popular in wealthy subdivisions and shopping malls throughout the Southwest. Connected to the old mining town below by a spectacular gondola, Mountain Village is a gated community with no visible need for gates. Protected against intruders by its high property values, an active police force, and the general inaccessibility of a planned vacation area at nine thousand feet above sea level, with one road in and one road out, Mountain Village is a man-made paradise for doctors and dentists, Texas oilmen, California property hunters, and other wealthy types who love to ski but can't afford their own mountain, a likely setting for a skewed postmodern version of F. Scott Fitzgerald's short story "The Ice Palace." Skiers can ride black diamond trials from early morning to late afternoon in relative isolation, and then head down from the slopes to the sliding doors of their condos. Those in the mood for after-ski nourishment can gulp down teriyaki bowls while listening to stoner tracks by Bob Marley and the Wailers, whose eyes would have likely bugged out of their heads at the sight of so much perfect white snow.

Jim Hogue was planning to make his home in Mountain Village, in a condo provided by Dr. Louis Alaia. A skier and local real estate developer, Dr. Alaia is a pleasant, grandfatherly man with thick white hair and olive-tan Mediterranean features that look out of place in the winter landscape. When I met him for lunch at his home, he was wearing a thick navy cashmere sweater. His gentle, absentminded manner betrays a singular degree of

involvement in his own thoughts and a corresponding lack of attention to large clues that other people may not be exactly what
they seem: he is a mark, a living, walking, breathing study in the
self-delusion that afflicts the victims of a con.

Dr. Alaia's condominium apartment is a temple to skiing, with
pictures of skiers on the walls, and skis and ski boots propped up
against the sliding glass doors through which we can watch skiers
heading down the slopes. We shared toasted tuna fish sandwiches and tomato soup for lunch. He approaches the details of
the Hogue case with the same obsessive nature that he brings to
his discussion of property values in Telluride. Somehow, his obsession with Telluride real estate and Jim Hogue's story merge
together in his mind, in a way that seems at first like a symptom
of mental confusion. As I stay with it, the two stories merge together in a way that reveals greater synchronicities at work.

"Did I tell you about the sofa chairs?" Alaia wondered.
Hunched over his bowl of tomato soup, he lifts another spoonful
to his mouth, and then continues his story.

"Jim was our property manager from 2003 until the beginning
of 2006, and so for two and a half, almost three years, he man-
aged this condo for us. He would take care of it for a nominal fee.
We turned down a sixty-thousand-dollar asking price for a parking space for this condo when we bought it, because I figured I
could do better things with sixty thousand," he explained, laying
his soup spoon down on the table. Like fantasists, or liars, obses-
sives are a particular kind of person. Normal conversation makes
their skin itch, until finally, the hour gets late, and the other
guests falter, and then they are free to talk about the one subject
that is actually worth caring about, and which is big enough to encompass the universe. He fidgeted for a moment before resum-
ing his pitch.

"And take the gondola. I mean, it's right there. So why blow
sixty thou? Anyway, realizing that in the interval, parking spaces

went up to over a hundred thousand dollars in value, I'm thinking, well, if I build this project, one of the ways that I'm gonna
sell it is if I give parking spaces to people, so why not give them
two?" he said. The immediate subject of Dr. Alaia's obsession is a
$20 million dollar condo project that he is shepherding to com-
pletion in Mountain Village. Jim was Dr. Alaia's right-hand man.
When they met, Jim was doing work for Alaia's neighbor,
Sheila Murphy, who owned and then sold the condo next door.
"He told me that he was a distance runner, and that he loved to
run, that he'd been in the Olympic trials," Dr. Alaia remembers.
"Oh yes, and that he was a chemical engineer, and that he had got
his chemical engineering degree from the University of Texas.
Which, of course, was totally untrue." As he talks about Hogue it
is clear that Dr. Alaia's mind is still confused about which parts of
Hogue's biography are real, and which are fiction. "My presump-
tion was that he came to Telluride and fell in love with the place,"
he told me. "He spent a couple of years in Italy, which I also don't
think is true."

Hogue and the Alaias soon fell into a comfortable routine,
with Hogue managing their condo and doing repairs, and helping out paying guests when they were away. When the family
came to town, they took Hogue out to dinner. "He was like a father figure I think to Jim, really," Dr. Alaia's wife, Susan, recalled.
I asked how his bond with Jim developed.

"Well, there you hit the nail on the head," Dr. Alaia said. "You
must remember that all this time, lot thirty-one was sitting there
with trees on it, doing nothing. I had spent all of my time doing
the due diligence on that, three single-family detached condominium lots, ski-in/ski-out right across the road. The double cab-
ins run right in the face of Oprah Winfrey's old house."

If it is hard sometimes to figure out what Dr. Alaia is talking
about, it is clear that Hogue saw him as a meal ticket and suc-

ceeded in ingratiating himself in the hopes of getting a piece of the development for himself. After hiring a local architect named Jerry Ross to do the plans, Alaia began using Hogue as a contractor, paying him small sums of money here and there. After a while, Hogue began putting more pressure on Alaia to provide him with a steady income while he waited for his free condo. Sometimes Jim rented out the Alaias' condo and pocketed the proceeds. Around town, they began to see him in the company of the Eastern European girls who worked in the shops and bars. When they came back home once they found their bed covered in dog hair. Another time, they found multiple long-distance calls on their phone.

"He got me those skis at a swap meet, though," Dr. Alaia recalled, pointing to a pair of nice skis leaning against the wall. "I would have had to pay six hundred bucks for those skis in L.A. without the bindings. I love them, they're great skis. So you know, I have to give him credit for that." Susan rolled her eyes.

There were strange holes in the stories Hogue told. For example, one time the Alaias' niece came to visit. Because she was a horsewoman, they thought she would get along well with Jim, who spoke of having grown up on a ranch. Instead, Jim avoided her. "He never talked about horses—said what kind of horse do you like, where did you ride," Susan Alaia remembered. Hogue brought over a copy of the FLEX exam, the test that foreign doctors take to become certified in the U.S. He had obtained a copy of the test, he said, for his girlfriend in Russia, who was a doctor.

"He was going through the questions, he read one to me, and asked me if I knew the answer," Dr. Alaia recalled. Hogue seemed upset when Dr. Alaia answered a question correctly. "I felt a note of dejection in his voice that I knew the answer and he didn't," he said. Of course, Dr. Alaia added, there was no reason why Hogue should have known the answers to the questions on the test, since he was not a doctor and had never been to medical school.

Living in Telluride is the fulfillment of Dr. Alaia's lifelong dream of endless mornings and afternoons on the slopes, and also perhaps of acceptance into a private club. His heroes are the local developers who had the vision to turn a busted-out mining town into a ski resort. Through his enthusiasm, it is possible to fall in love with the vision they sold him of endless sunny winter mornings and afternoons in the Rockies—a California of the slopes. "I was here the day the ski area opened on December 7, 1972," he said, pointing to a framed newspaper clipping on the wall. When I tease him about being a closet hippie, he smiles the inward smile of a lifelong introvert whose high intelligence and skills had combined with a shy nature to isolate him from normal human companionship and to lose himself in work and hobbies. Listening to him talk about Telluride is like listening to an old man's memories of a pretty girl he kissed when he was young.

"I was a practicing orthopedic surgeon, heavily into joint re- placement in Southern California," he said, remembering what it was like to be a successful surgeon with his own private clinic. "One of the things that brought me to California was the fact that I was a boater and a skier and I could do both in the same week. In fact, one of the first weeks I came out here, I went skiing one day and water-skiing the other day. I happened to subscribe to something called the *Kiplinger Letter.* And one day, I saw an ad about Walt Disney putting up the Mineral King resort. I still have the posters for Disney's Mineral King task force in my garage. I can't bear to throw them away," he added as his eyes mist over. He paused for a moment before he continued on.

The Mineral King boosters were led by a plastics engineer named Hap Wood who had some connections to Disney, who helped lobby the forest service to let Disney establish a ski area. Ronald Reagan, before he became governor of California, got the pass for the road to go into Mineral King. "I skied it twice by helicopter. The skis I skied it with are still in the closet," Dr. Alaia said, pausing again. "I am not sure why I get emotional about that. But anyway, I was president of Mineral King Ski Club in 1972, happily, just for a couple of years, and we made those two trips into Mineral King by helicopter. It was very rewarding. Disney gave us an animated movie with drawings from their artists of what the resort would look like, and we set up a booth at the Ski Expo in October 1972."

Mineral King never became the world-class ski resort of Dr. Alaia's dreams. At the 1972 California Ski Expo, the doctor in search of the perfect ski condo met Joe Zolene, the visionary resort promoter who would bring him to Telluride. The California Ski Expo is a disorienting place, a perfect setting for lost characters to embark on weird schemes while suffering from bouts of severe dissociation. Convention-goers exited the 80 degree heat and fortress-like riot-control architecture of downtown Los Angeles and entered the great hall of the Los Angeles Convention Center, where they were greeted by a giant plastic mountain that looked vaguely like snow. Ski-world celebrities were regularly flown in by the equipment manufacturers, and famous skiers like Jean-Claude Killy attempted desultory stunts. Warren Miller movies, the samizdat chronicles of the freestyle ski culture, were projected on giant screens above the convention-center floor while salesmen for Rossignol and Salomon sold expensive skis and boots to natives of Los Angeles, many of whom had never seen actual snow.

It was at the Ski Expo that Dr. Alaia, then one of Southern California's leading joint-replacement specialists, met Joe Zolene, William Barron Hilton's lawyer, who had a ranch out in Aspen, a fast-growing ski town where property was becoming unaffordable for the casual skier. Zolene had enough clout to get a Swiss group to put in the towers for the chair-lift in the summer of 1972, and to raise an additional $6 million, which was not quite enough to realize his dream of turning Telluride into the next Aspen. "He said, 'Listen, I'm flying up next week, why don't you join me?' " Dr. Alaia remembered. "So I did, and one thing led to another, I bought a couple of his condos, and became good friends, and. . . ." His voice trailed off.

Dr. Alaia has been a sucker all his life for other men's schemes—the joke here being that being a sucker has made him rich. As a kid growing up in New Rochelle, he used to ski down the hill in front of his house and on the local golf course on a pair of old skis with bear-trap bindings that his parents gave him for his birthday when he was seventeen. After putting his skis away during medical school, he got hooked again while doing his residency in orthopedics at the Albert Einstein College of Medicine in the Bronx. "Every time I was off, I would race up to Vermont, ski for the weekend," he remembered. He would drive two hundred miles up to ski Killington or Bromley or his favorite, Mount Snow. For a while, he considered buying a condo up at Mammoth Lakes. When he saw Telluride, he was hooked.

"There were no traffic lights, no chain franchises and all that," he remembered. "I was reading about the Yellowstone Club in Wyoming—that's supposed to be a private ski area for multimillionaires," he explained. "And I kept thinking, 'Boy, I'd like to meet one of them and tell him, you know, I don't know if you're a loner or a hermit or whatever, you really ought to come here, because this is a true private ski area.' "

In the early 1970s, a large banner hung over Colorado Avenue, the main drag in downtown Telluride, that neatly summarized the mixed attitudes of the hippies towards the suckers. Decorated in psychedelic lettering designed to catch the attention of even the most zonked-out stoner, the banner read, "Don't Hassle the Turkeys." The hippies were happy to have the skiers in town because skiers meant cash. At the same time, they looked down their noses at the future condo owners like Dr. Alaia. He bought a place in town, and Zolene took him under his wing. He sold him a few more condos, and gave him lifetime ski passes for his children, Mark and Maria.

"Joe Zolene used to talk about Mountain Village, and I used to think, well, that's not the name of the town. He's just thinking that there's gonna be a mountain village here! He envisioned that," he added, shaking his head with the wonder that one man could imagine an entire town in his head. It was Zolene who first envisioned building a new town on top of the mountain, and connecting the new town to the mining area below by a gondola. When he went broke and lost the ski area in 1978, Dr. Alaia bought the great man's ranch, which he later sold at a profit.

As Dr. Alaia told me the story of Telluride, Susan busied herself with clearing the remains of our tuna fish sandwiches. "He refinishes cabinets and does flooring work," she added in, over the sound of running water, as Dr. Alaia stared at the expanse of blinding white snow outside his sliding door. "Just give him a book that shows him how, and he's got the intellect to do it."

"The only reason I don't own a table saw is because I'm a surgeon," Dr. Alaia abruptly interjected, in the off-kilter style to which I am beginning to become accustomed. "I have had to fix too many guys who've lopped off things with a table saw. Also, I had to retire from surgery because of narcolepsy." I don't mean to give him a strange look, but I do. "I enjoyed working with wood," he added, before finally bringing the conversation back around to James Hogue. "So there was a camaraderie between me and him. Because the kid is a master carpenter."

Susan rolled her eyes again. "I haven't sat down and looked at the DSM, but he probably fits the criteria for an antisocial personality disorder," she said. It is a conversation they have had many times before. I asked Dr. Alaia if, to the best of his knowledge, Hogue had any actual training or certification as a carpenter. He shook his head, then gave me a quizzical look. "He probably got some formal training when he was in jail, for all I know," he answered.

The arrangement between the absentminded mark and the metaphysically oriented con man might have gone on for years, but reality finally intervened. When Hogue was on the run, he began sending Dr. Alaia e-mails requesting payment for back wages. The police gave Alaia a program that would allow them to track the e-mails, which became less pleasant as time went on.

"Dear Lou, Here is my itemized listing of work with the Tramontana project, over 116 weeks. I am sure that I missed a lot, and always underestimated when not certain. I think that this is a pretty fair assessment, and it is much lower than I previously thought," the first letter began.

For thirty hours of "site visits" and another forty hours of meetings, eighty hours of "interior design," including a trip to Denver to look at tile, and over two hundred hours of itemized phone calls, Hogue asked for a bit over $12,000, which seemed fair enough. He asked that the money be wired to account #13848748 at the Citibank branch at 757 Madison Avenue in New York. By the time Hogue added a postscript to his letter, the strain was palpable: "Of course, I could really use the payment ASAP, molto urgente, as I am trying to protect my assets as much as possible. Please keep me posted. Thanks, Jim."

A letter sent a few days later, on Friday, January 13, 2006, appeared to be written by a person operating under heavy strain.

"Dear Lou," the letter began.

> Best not to bother with FedEx and just wire to Citibank. I can't imagine trying to figure mileage for anything more distant than yesterday; I don't think that I can remember what I had for breakfast then.

The letter continues:

> Two maintenance notes for K4; the central floor outlet in the living room seems to have gone dead and resetting the breaker doesn't work. The wireless will probably have to be moved to another power source. Also, the lights in the master tub seem to be burning out at an alarming rate; the last one survived only a few weeks. Maybe there is a surge, or just a randomly short-lived bulb. My bet is that there is something wrong with the wiring.
>
> Take care, Jim

III. William Purdy

Exiting Dr. Alaia's condo, I was dazzled by the sunstruck whiteness of the Mountain Village slopes and the bouncy reggae music pumping from outdoor speakers. I took my cell phone out of my pocket and called Sheriff Bill Masters at the San Miguel County jail, and asked if I could speak to James Hogue. It is a request I have made before, on the phone and also in writing. Masters is an upbeat, plainspoken person. "We've discussed the matter with Mr. Hogue and he's refusing to speak to you," Masters said, in his cheerful way.

I took the gondola down 1,250 feet to Telluride, and walked through the snow until I reached the corner of West Galena and North Oak, where I met a handyman named William Purdy, who was Hogue's next-door neighbor. I will be able to find the house where he is working, he said, because his truck will be parked in the driveway, and because no one is home at any of the other houses on the block. Purdy reminds me of a character in a Robert Mitchum movie from the 1950s—not Mitchum himself, but a secondary character, a wannabe tough guy with a bad upbringing who steals a horse or forces a girl and then gets shot or beat up by Robert Mitchum in the first fifteen minutes of the movie. He was wearing a white T-shirt, his black hair was slicked back on his head with a Brylcreem-like substance, and he was talking on a silver Razr flip phone—a modern addition to the picture. A dusty bison head sat on the floor behind him, below a reproduction of a Chamonix Mont-Blanc ski poster from the 1920s.

"Tell me some basic stuff, like how old you are," I asked him. He stared at me for a moment, taking my measure.

"I'm forty-five. Right now," he answered, staring me right in the eye. The Mitchum look is part of his act. He is the town gossip, a role he plays for kicks in a low-key, vaguely sinister way. Purdy wouldn't hurt a fly. His daughter, who won't tell me how old she is but appears to be about ten, has apparently invented a fever in order to skip school. She sits in a chair in the living room, watching a movie on her father's laptop. They moved out here together in 1995. Before coming to Telluride, Purdy worked at Mount Baldy, a small mountain town outside Los Angeles where Purdy shoveled snow. "It's a little box-canyon town that I loved, but I had a dispute with the ski area where I worked, and so I kind of ran away," he offered. "I went up to Canada, up the Pacific Coast, and then I came here. It's like Mount Baldy with money. There was always a cash-flow problem in Mount Baldy. There was never enough snow."

"You went to England!" his daughter exclaimed.

Purdy shrugged. "I saw the beauty and I said, rich people are gonna have to buy their way into beauty, because the world's getting more congested," he explained.

"When did you move out near Jim?" I asked him.

"Actually, Jim moved up near me," Purdy said. His daughter was getting bored.

"Can I watch my show?" she asked.

"Someday you're going to remember that your dad told a long story to a strange man who was wearing a sweatshirt with a big black dog on it," I told her. Purdy nodded.

"Baby, this is why you were sick today," he explained. I asked him why he moved up near San Bernardo.

"It was right in the middle of my plow route. I'm not into the Telluride beauty crap. I'm into bread and butter, okay?"

I wonder whether he might occasionally be moved by the sunlight on the mountains, or the stars at night. He shook his head no, and then only relents a bit. "I think it's nice that I can make good money living here. But I could give a rat's ass about natural beauty," he insisted.

His daughter looked up from her video screen. "He likes his job a lot," she said. Purdy nodded. "I like my job a lot," he agreed. I asked him what kind of people are attracted to beautiful places.

"People who have a dark side," he said. His daughter laughed at something on her screen. Purdy warmed to his subject. As he spoke, I began to see him less as a character from a black-and-white movie and more like a real person, whose demons might be real. The way William Purdy deals with his demons is by making jokes.

"When our dark side owns us, maybe we look outside of ourselves to deal with it, you know," he said. James Hogue was swallowed by his dark side a long time ago. "I got into this bizarre conversation with him one time on a hiking trail," he remembered. Hogue's weirdness reminds him of his father, who was a civil engineer. "I asked him, 'Do you have your bachelor's in civil engineering?' And he said, 'No, my master's.' "

The conversation was weird not only because Hogue was lying about being an engineer but also because he was stealing electricity from Purdy's house, a fact that he had discovered when he came home early from a trip and found Hogue running a heavy yellow extension cord from the outside of Purdy's house into the workshop he kept on the first floor. "Right outside his window are forty amps of plugs. So he'd plug in," Purdy recalled. "And I go, 'What are you doing?' And he said, 'It's there! I am short on power. It's there. I just need a little more power.' He had his landlord, Mark, convinced that he was involved with a lady back east, and that he was a custom woodworker and that he built fancy wood boxes," he sighed.

"He's a liar," William Purdy's daughter said.

Her father thought about what she said for a few seconds before answering, "Well, he never did a thing."

"He went to jail," his daughter said.

Purdy nodded. "Another funny thing about him was he used to carry gas cans around on top of his truck," he said. It was common knowledge in town that Hogue would siphon gas from people's cars, which was a special inconvenience to his victims in the winter.

"He loved to steal from the people he was closest to," Purdy said. "I knew he'd gone through my house, gone through my stuff. But he didn't steal from me, other than the power and the gasoline. He would do these pilgrimages to somewhere, and he would pack everything. He was fully loaded. So maybe he was giving offerings to somebody. You know, maybe he had some other life where he was a hero. He lived in the cold. He never heated the house. He was superior about living in the cold. He would burn a fire now and again, and I found out later that he was water-dripping. It keeps the pipes from freezing."

When I asked Purdy to explain Hogue's behavior, he had a ready answer.

"I think he got off on manipulating people," he said.

I suggested that Hogue enjoyed being a made-up person, a fictional character. He wanted to become unreal.

"I think he liked the fact that people would believe him. Maybe he didn't believe anybody. I think he really got excited about the fact that people trusted him, and that he was violating that trust," Purdy explained. In the backyard of his house, where I have already been twice, without Purdy's knowledge, I noticed a number of snowplows as well as a school bus and a taxicab. He makes money by letting them park there, he offered, registering the fact that I have been prowling around his yard. The thing is, he continued, that Jim wanted to get caught.

"He did?" his daughter asked. No longer interested in her movie, she has pulled up a chair. She is used to being taken seriously by her father.

"He wasn't taking things to make money," Purdy explained. "He wanted to violate people's trust. He kept everything in his house! He stole gas from every house in the neighborhood where he lives, and he drives around with gas cans on top of his truck! And then he says, with a straight face, 'I don't understand what's going on.' That's the way he would respond. Cold sober. It is funny," he admitted.

Jim used to appear in runner's tights at all hours of the day, even in extreme cold weather, and run. He never got up early in the morning, although he always said he did. Purdy could tell because the lights in his house were never on. He never used to heat his house. Once, snow fell from the roof and hit the pipe on his propane tank and broke it, Purdy said. "Propane is explosive. Propane goes downhill. We all run on propane. So I smelled gas behind my house for a couple of days. That was the only thing that I was really pissed off about. My kid's bedroom's right there. It could have caused a problem."

When things got hot, Hogue's behavior became even more erratic, Purdy remembered. He shuttled trash bags full of stolen goods from his truck to his house, and from his house to the truck.

"Oh, no, no, no," he said, when I ask him whether he felt living next to Hogue was dangerous. "He was harmless. Was it sad? Was it funny? I would say yes to both. I mean, it's a very sad story about a man."

His daughter nodded. "He wanted to go to jail," she said.

"He was always totally harmless, he just didn't respect privacy," Purdy said.

All of us have the potential to spin out, Purdy told me. Jim spun out. Another way of looking at Jim's situation is that he was a type of pervert who specialized in property crimes. He really liked breaking down people's boundaries. "I should be careful," Purdy added. "I have a big mouth. He's not a bad person. He's damaged goods. I just think he's hurting deeply inside, and when you're hurting, you go to jail. We all have this dark side, and he's living it." I like William Purdy.

"He's part of us!" he declaimed. "We're all in this together, Republican, Democrat, blue, green, yellow, whatever. Go to L.A. Go to Wal-Mart," he said, jabbing his thick finger at the wall, to indicate the greater craziness of the world beyond. "The employees, they talk to themselves while they're stacking boxes in the aisles. Mental illness in America is fantastic. People take a look around them, and maybe they look twice. Then they freak out and shut down for life."

IV. Christmas Is the Biggest Lie

The road out to Jim's house on East San Bernardo on the outskirts of Telluride is one of the most beautiful drives in the Rockies. The beauty of these mountains is hardly a secret, but still there is no describing it correctly. The near-paralyzing effect of the sunlit mountains on the naked eye might be explained by the fact that these are some of the highest habitable mountains in the world. Driving through the high mountain passes of the Rockies is like traveling through a wormhole into geological time. The sheer faces of ice and rock, the blinding reflection of the sunlight off the white snow, accord with Romantic ideas of the sublime in a way that combines with a lack of accustomed levels of oxygen to create a high-order giddiness; can lead to flights of abstraction; and are made pleasurable in an unexpected way by the warmth that settles inside your chest. Once you are here, in Telluride, there is no especially convincing reason to be anywhere else. Skiing these mountains is a way to be held aloft on the wings of angels. In even more perfect and terrifying moments, staring off into the abyss that rushes up to embrace you at the edge of a sheer rock cliff, you can touch the face of God. A few miles before I reached Jim's cabin I looked up and saw the most perfect mountain within a hundred miles, Wilson's Peak, which is over fourteen thousand feet high and is best known as the mountain on the Coors Light beer cans. It is hard to imagine a mountain anywhere in the world that could sell more beer than Wilson's Peak.

Patrick Kurtz has a view of the Rockies out the window of his office. His custom woodshop, where we meet one afternoon for a few hours, is across the street from Jim's house. Patrick has gray hair and the peppy, ultra-caffeinated manner of a reformed ski bum who sobered up and now works hard for a living. He is wearing a blue Carhartt workman's jacket, a red ski hat, and a pair of dark sunglasses on a string around his neck. He moved here from Iowa, after going to the University of Denver. He is also a real carpenter, having joined the union when he was still a kid in Des Moines.

"I guess when the robbery happened is when I met him," he said. One Friday morning, he came into work and noticed that the rocks that he had placed on top of a tarp outside were missing, and that the load of rare Honduran mahogany beneath the tarp appeared to have been depleted. "A good-sized kitchen's worth," Kurtz's partner, James Guest added. "It was for a job in town, at the Oak Street Inn. The whole place was Honduran mahogany." Hogue was spotted taking boards from the pile by a worker, who described the runner's slight build and the clothes he habitually wore in the winter.

Kurtz called the police with Hogue's license plate number. The next morning, one of his workers called from Trout Lake, a nearby nature reserve, where he saw Hogue's truck parked near a Forest Service shed. "He saw him walking down the road with a hoodie on, trying to look inconspicuous," he remembered. "And so I said, 'Call the police right now.' And that was the last time anyone saw him up here before he got arrested down in Arizona."

By coincidence or not, Guest went cross-country skiing later that afternoon near Trout Lake, where he saw a pile of ski boots and other gear under an old water tower. There was another pile of stuff further down the road. The police were already there. A week later, they invited Kurtz and Guest across the street to visit Jim's house. In the kitchen, they saw cases of wine and champagne. On the shelves of Hogue's bedroom upstairs were what appeared to be family pictures, some of which turned out to be

Photoshopped composites. In a secret room in the basement, concealed behind a refrigerator, Kurtz and Guest found their Honduran mahogany. "There was just like this cavity," Kurtz remembered. "There were these super-expensive old photographs of the Indians in this area. Super-pricey stuff. And then, there was all of our lumber, piled up super-neat."

I asked Patrick whether he agreed with the thesis that Jim Hogue only stole from rich people, who deserved it.

"Nah, I never felt that way about him," he said. "His drug of choice was stealing. It sounds like he's been doing it most of his life."

We talked for a while, and then I put on my jacket and my Princeton ski hat and went outside, where I stood for a while in the snow before I crossed the one-way street and made my way to Hogue's house, a simple pinewood A-frame cabin next door to William Purdy. A rustic mountain shack like this, half an hour outside of Telluride, might cost north of $400,000, which isn't a lot for this neighborhood. I had lived in a few houses like it, none of them in the Rockies or with such gorgeous scenery. It's the place where Nick Carraway would come to live after his quickie marriage to Jordan Baker didn't pan out.

Hogue didn't care much for telling stories about himself. He wanted other people to tell stories about him. His voice was in my head because I had been listening to tapes of our prior conversations, which had recently been forwarded to me by a lawyer, who had been holding them as evidence in a case that I am not allowed to talk about or write about here. What struck me was his modest way of speaking, his soft, quiet voice, never volunteering more information than was absolutely necessary. He had a habit of using the word "little" in a way that casually diminished whatever he was talking about. It made him feel bigger to think of other people as small. You had to listen to him speak for hours before you got the point. Their little parties. Their little Thanks-

giving. Their little Christmas. Their little Nude Olympics they
had in the snow.

At first, Hogue's distinctive habit of attaching diminishing
modifiers to varied objects and facets of existence seemed like a
preppy affectation meant to signify that he was a humble person
who was not easily impressed. He lived in a world of things that
were small. Yet he was not so humble or distracted that he didn't
spend time and energy making judgments about the lives of
others. Occasionally, a darker, more aggressive presence made
itself felt in his language, insisting that he was the smartest
and strongest person in the room. He embraced a higher and
more challenging form of existence, on a more elevated, abstract
plane.

In the back of the house was a big yard that bloomed in spring-
time with red-stick willows and cottonwoods, and a lovely stand
of aspen trees, which grow here like weeds. On the first level of
his house was a long garage-like room with a concrete floor
where he set up his woodshop, in which he made cabinets and
did custom work for the apartments he renovated in town. He
kept his stolen pictures and paintings in the secret room where
he hid Kurtz's mahogany. On top of the garage-like structure was
a wood-sided A-frame made out of pine, with a satellite dish
clinging precariously to the sharply pitched roof. An external
staircase led up to the living quarters in the crook of the frame,
protected from the elements by a cantilevered overhang sup-
ported by a thick wooden beam. Beneath the living quarters, the
first floor kept going another forty feet into the back yard.

Here, in the Rockies, with sheep-like mountains rising behind
his wreck of a cottage, with the windows long shut and rusted-out
siding rising halfway up the bare concrete foundation, he found a
landscape that matched the magnificent abstraction he found inside his own head. I understood how he felt because there were
times when diminishing the size of everything around me was the

only way I could find to protect my ego. When you let go, and the
world around you expands back to its normal size, you discover
that the world is a lot bigger than you remembered it, and that
you are alone.

I had a good idea of what the house looked like inside. On the
hook near the door was a black leather jacket with a Dead
Kennedys patch and a variety of rude punk emblems. The CDs
were more his taste: Dave Brubeck and Nat King Cole, collec-
tions of Christmas music, recordings of the *Carmina Burana* and
The Magic Flute, a John Coltrane box set, and a box set of gospel
music called *Testify!* The Western-themed books on his shelves
had titles like *The Endurance* and *The Eternal Frontier.* On the
shelves was a copy of *The Complete Idiot's Guide to Learning
Russian.* There were yellow Post-it notes with the Russian words
for "window" and "door" and "stove." The windows were covered
with cheap printed cotton tapestries. The floors were clean but
littered with athletic equipment. In the center of the living room
was a Southwestern-style leather wing chair. In the bedroom was
a VCR, a television set, and a shelf of DVDs including *L.A. Con-
fidential, Charmed,* and *East-West* that he had found in other
people's homes. There were fresh boxes of New Balance running
shoes, and nineteenth-century snuff boxes painted with charm-
ing woodland scenes.

Few if any of the things in the house had originally belonged to
him. The polished copper pots that hung from the ceiling were
stolen, though to his credit he knew how to use them. He had
a friend in Las Vegas who had been a chef. A floor-to-ceiling
bookshelf was filled with cookbooks including *How to Cook
Everything, A New Way to Cook, Beer-Can Chicken,* and the
Moosewood Restaurant Daily Special cookbook. Above the sink
in the kitchen, with its drop-dead-gorgeous view of snow-
covered mountains, was a copy of the *Principles of Internal Medicine* and a Cleveland baseball cap with a grinning Indian-head

logo. There was also a stack of books in Russian. He kept five pairs of Dalbello ski boots in the hallway near the closet, along with a set of Dansk china that looked like a gift from someone else's wedding. His goal went beyond simple theft. He was aiming to assemble a new self out of the bits and pieces of other people's lives. "This is a genuine antique engraving guaranteed to be more than 100 years old Framed 27 Cecil Court London," read the fine print on a colorful portrait of a blue-hooded parakeet. The claim that it was a "genuine engraving" had probably struck him as funny. Hanging from the ceiling was a collection of fancy Panama hats that he used to hide his advancing middle-aged baldness, which made it difficult for him to continue to claim that he was twenty-six or twenty-nine. There were scattered pictures of Hogue with his Russian girlfriend, the doctor. There was a clumsily Photoshopped picture of Hogue in a red cashmere sweater with his arm around a different girl whom I could not identify.

The detectives had also documented the inside of Jim's pantry and the refrigerator, which turned out to contain a single yogurt container, low-fat Philadelphia cream cheese, a plastic envelope of Horizon organic cheese sticks, and a dozen bottles of Dom Pérignon. In the closet were bags of Doritos and Lays potato chips and cans of Pepsi.

In a storage locker in nearby Fort Garland were building materials that looked like they were intended for a house—window frames, a skylight, lighting fixtures, plastic pipes. There were also rugs, boxes of skin-firming cream, expensive skis, a Bob Carver subwoofer, an awful blue-tinted lithograph of winter morning light over high mountains that may have been the Rockies, and a painting of a stag in the mountains, awkwardly balanced on its hind legs, as though the artist had more experience painting people or dogs. Even in his crazy state, Jim had enough taste to put this stuff in storage. There was a carousel horse with thinning handfuls of genuine horsehair plastered to its scalp. There was a mounted mountain lion head, a pair of moose antlers, the head of a deer, a snowboard, a tennis racquet, a fax machine, and several power drills. There were two Burton Cruzer 145 snowboards. There were more kinds of crap than you could shake a stick at.

The longer I live, the more of my friends from college settle into patterns of behavior that make no sense except as the outcome of internal pressures and forces that lock them into ways of thinking and behaving that would have caused them to look on in horrified disbelief when they were eighteen or twenty-nine. They get married. They have kids. They gain thirty pounds, and dress in expensive, brightly colored clothing. I am talking about myself here, but I could say worse things about almost any one of my friends. In my heart, I think of what happened to Jim as what could easily have happened to any smart, sensitive person who was more than a little unbalanced, which is to say that given the right circumstances any one of us might wake up one morning severed from some essential and sustaining feeling of connection to the universe. We would find ourselves lost in a dark forest with no way to escape except by becoming someone new.

Another notable fact about James Hogue that can be established beyond even a shadow of doubt is that he had a peculiar lifelong fixation on Christmas. He hoarded albums of Christmas music both sacred and profane, from liturgical classics to recordings by Nat King Cole, the Beach Boys, and the Pretenders. Christmas was his favorite day of the year.

The Hogue family made a special point of celebrating the holiday like no other day on the calendar, with large helpings of Christmas ham and turkey, and side dishes of potatoes and sauerkraut, in memory of the family's German roots. There is footage of Jim's mother, Maria, playing the piano on Christmas with a dopey, miraculous grin stretched across her face, the same irrepressible grin that would cross Jim's face whenever he thought about his favorite holiday. So widely shared is the Christmas mystery among even the most secular-seeming American households that few people neglect to pay homage to the family-oriented demands of the holiday, which is that everyone comes home at least once a year and pretends to live out a storybook version of ideals of domestic harmony and generational interconnectedness which hearken back to the dimly remembered experiences of grandparents and great-grandparents who grew up in much more family-oriented societies than ours a century or more ago. Children wake up on Christmas morning to find that their year-long prayers for new bikes and dolls have been answered and rush to compare notes with their friends.

In most American families, Christmas is a masquerade that begins when children are very young and in which adults are often more invested than the children for whose benefit the festivities are often aranged. Christmas is a child's first introduction to lying, beginning with recitals of the lie of Santa Claus and extending to the pantomime of perfect familial relations that are hardly replicated on the other three hundred and sixty-four days of the year. Christmas is the ultimate American holiday, not because we are a Christian country, but because it is the annual spectacular culmination of our ardent national desire to wake up every morning brand new.

Hogue's mother, Maria, grew up in Scotts Bluff, Nebraska, as a member of one of the rural German communities that lived in relative isolation amid the prejudice of many of their neighbors in the years before, during, and after the First World War. For all her intelligence, it was easy to get Maria's goat, and her children, her husband, and her grandchildren all indulged in the sport of winding her up by contradicting something she previously said, or saying something that she might regard as strange. She met Jim's father, Eugene Hogue, while the two of them worked as shipping clerks for the Union Pacific railroad in Kansas City, tracking the progress of freight cars across the Midwest. In private, Maria was lively, opinionated, high-strung, and frankly a bit odd. Gene was a former college runner with a sly, deadpan sense of humor who mostly kept quiet. In public, their roles were often reversed: Maria was the shy one, while Gene did most of the talking.

Yet while the marriage of two railroad shipping clerks might seem like a recipe for stability, the Hogue family had more than its share of secrets. Maria's two older daughters, Vicky and Theresa, had two different fathers, neither of whom was Gene Hogue. Vicky's father, Ross Rogers, was Maria's first husband. Theresa was born out of wedlock to a man whose name was not preserved in the family memory. The story the family told was that Vicky's father had been a Catholic, and that both the Catholic and the Lutheran clergy had advised the couple against marriage, because of the strain that conversion to another Christian denomination would place on the family. Faced with the refusal of either clergy to marry them, the couple split up, and Maria moved to Kansas City, where she met Gene, the son of a rancher named Arthur Hogue from Laramie, Wyoming. Remembered by his friends as a lover of winter sports, especially skiing, Arthur Hogue craved the wide-open spaces of the West. When he wasn't alone, he got married, to several different women, and was rumored to have enjoyed girlfriends on the side.

There was a streak of wildness, of rule-breaking, that ran deep on both sides of the family and that resisted the attempts of Gene and Maria to give their children a stable, happy life. Their first daughter, Betty, was indulged by both parents, and had early problems with drugs. One Christmas, she stole the $100 bills that her parents had given to each sibling, denied any responsibility for the act, and then spent the money on drugs. Eventually she descended into a spiral of addiction that led her to heroin. Living

off the charity of her parents, she made occasional forays into
prostitution and died young. Both Vicky and Theresa got di-
vorced, and also died young. Jim, the baby of the family, became
a runner like his father. Forced to take Betty running one afternoon by his parents, Jim hit her over the head with a tree branch
and left her bleeding in the forest. His parents called the police.

Theresa's son, Brian Patrick, who holds a PhD in biology from
Kent State University and was a particular favorite of Jim's, con-
trasted the slippery and utilitarian approach to reality that char-
acterized the Hogue family with his father's family, which was
more sober-minded and conservative. "The surface of the law
was really not something that was terribly important to anyone,"
he remembered. "It was just something intrinsic to the family.
They lived in a world that was very different from the world that I
grew up in."

By the late 1990s, Maria's world had unraveled completely. A
lifelong obsessive, she collected tin cans for her church, plunder-
ing the Dumpsters and trash cans of her neighborhood in North
Kansas City where she became such a familiar figure that people
left their cans out in plastic bags and made her gifts of clothes
and food. After the death of her husband, she began collecting
plastic take-out containers, newspapers, and other useful things
that her neighbors had unaccountably thrown away. When her
hot-water heater and refrigerator broke, she refused to allow a
path to be cleared through her hoardings, and chose to live in a
squalid mess of old food containers and eight-foot-high stacks of
magazines and newspapers with only a narrow pathway cleared
between the front door and her bed.

V. The Escape Artist

The idea of leaving your old life behind and becoming a new person is too deeply rooted in who we are to simply dismiss Hogue's behavior as one man's defective adaptation to reality, though it was also that. The disease that took over Jim Hogue's life might be diagnosed as a low-grade fever in tens of millions more. There is no shortage of people like James Hogue who walk among us disguised as people like ourselves, having made themselves up from scratch and then acquired credit cards and mortgages and spouses. The idea that we can be whoever we want to be, regardless of our origins, or the color of our skin, or the beliefs of our parents, is familiar to all of us as a grade-school homily. What James Hogue did with his life is deeply rooted in the Western religious tradition that holds that believers are born again in Christ and leave behind their prior, sinful nature. It's what our Founding Fathers did when they declared their independence from the authority of King George. Escaping from the burdens of the past and becoming a new person is part of the birthright of every American. It's a deeply disturbing and revolutionary fantasy about the malleability of the individual and the elasticity of fate that has transformed our idea of the past from the solid ground on which we stand into something airy and disposable.

To say that a lie deprives other people of their autonomy to act as fellow human beings is another rationalization of a preexisting moral schema that comes from your parents. No one forces you to listen to a lie. You listened to a lie, and believed the lie, according to your own mistaken apprehension of reality. For a while, Hogue's lies were entirely successful in pulling the wool over the

eyes of everyone he met, from racing bicycle manufacturers, to
property owners, fellow dreamers, teachers and administrators at
Ivy League colleges, the children of some of America's richest
and most socially prominent families, his fellow runners, to the
residents of Telluride, Colorado. A good part of his success in his
various endeavors came from his skill as a liar, a practice with
which all of us are in some ways familiar. Compared to you or me,
Jim is what might be called an advanced liar, meaning that he can
say all kinds of unlikely or impossible things and convince you
that they are true. He was so good a liar that he could lie with his
eyes, and with a word here and there, so that when you confronted him later on he could honestly say that he had never said
anything of the kind.[2]

2. Respected authorities on the subject of lying usually begin with the general
idea that telling lies is wrong, at least in most cases: they then proceed to explain
why and under what circumstances permission might be granted for an occasional lie or two, on the principle that any absolute prohibition against lying
would be inhuman or at least inhumane. One striking characteristic of this type
of argument is the ease with which dramatic examples of necessary lies ("a Nazi
officer knocks on your door, and demands to know if any Jews are hiding in your
house") give way to vague generalities like "peace," "social harmony," "justice,"
or "the greater good of the community" according to which many lies—perhaps
even most lies—might be seen as beneficial by someone, beginning with the liar
himself.
    The idea that lying is bad or wrong goes back at least to the ancient Greeks,
who believed that the truth was noble and lying was a low type of behavior that
cheapened one's character. Aristotle saw honesty as the midpoint between the
flaws of boastfulness and excessive humility, implying that one could lie by un-
derstatement just as significantly as through exaggeration. The Biblical texts of
the ancient Hebrews enjoined believers to "keep far from a false matter" (Exo-
dus 23:7) and not to "deal falsely nor lie to one another" (Leviticus 19:11). Contrary to uneducated modern belief, a prohibition against lying is not included
among the Ten Commandments handed down by God to Moses at Sinai, which
prohibit "bearing false witness against one's neighbor," a more circumscribed of-
fense. Talmudic sources and later rabbinic commentators pointed to over a
dozen lies told in the Biblical texts by Abraham, Aaron, and other major characters, including God himself, who lies to Sarah. The rabbis agreed that lying was
permissible in order to save a life and to preserve peace.
    The Catholic Church took an even more flexible approach to lying by identify-

It goes without saying that Jim's way of living made him dangerous to others, and would also qualify him as crazy according to most psychology textbooks. Yet to look on his choices as merely the symptoms of mental illness is to trivialize both the extent and the nature of his misdeeds, and also the troubled idea that he latched on to, the common shorthand for which is the American Dream. His lies were part of a game that he played

---

ing the wrong of a lie with the social damage that it caused, implying that lies could be excused depending on their visible effects. For the medieval Catholic philosopher Thomas Aquinas, lies were wrong because they caused damage to individuals and to society: the harm caused by a lie was therefore understood as being external to the lie itself. Immanuel Kant insisted that lying weakens the common bonds of trust that hold society together. The German Protestant theologian Dietrich Bonhoeffer, who was hanged by the Nazis at the Flossenbürg concentration camp after joining a plot to kill Hitler, argued that lying was a natural inclination that we struggle to unlearn. Truth-telling, Bonhoeffer believed, is a learned behavior that we undertake in order to give the truthfulness that we owe to God some practical form in the world.

The one great exception to the often slippery philosophical and theological discussion of lying is Augustine of Hippo, the most significant writer of late antiquity. In *De Mendacio*—written in part to counter the Priscillian heresy, a gnostic belief that insisted among other things that believers were not obligated to tell the truth to strangers—Augustine defined a lie in the lasting way that would be adopted by philosophers and theologians from Aquinas to Bonhoeffer: "A lie consists in speaking a falsehood with the intention of deceiving." While Augustine's definition of lying is the basis for almost every subsequent piece of serious writing on the subject, few thinkers before or since have been willing to concur with Augustine's absolute prohibition on all forms of lying no matter how dire the results of telling the truth might be. As a writer, and a flawed believer in the Augustinian approach to truth, I find the absence of any general agreement with Augustine quite puzzling.

Counterpoising the idea of an inner man against the public claims of the Roman Empire, Augustine invented the idea of interiority that writers and psychiatrists in the West take as the universal component of human nature. "In the inward person dwells truth." For Augustine, lying is destructive of language, which is the basis of human solidarity. Telling the truth to strangers was part of the foundation of any human community. The seriousness with which Augustine took his prohibition on lying can be judged by the fact that he did allow circumstances where killing and war were permissible, but never lying.

with reality. The person who was hurt the most by his lies was
Jim Hogue. He never hurt anyone physically. He always paid his
bills on time.

Even those of us who try very hard never to lie can probably
recall at least one or two slips on the path of our otherwise truth-
loving existence. Just as our social arrangements depend on the
sharing of accurate information, so too do they rely on the activ-

---

Telling lies was absolutely wrong, Augustine believed, because it created a
conscious split between one's inner self and the representation that one makes
of oneself in the world through language. A lie is a perversion of language that
splits a person in half. The evil proper to lying is doubleness—lying divides the
inner self and corrupts the medium with which the self connects to others and to
God. The morally significant consequences of a lie therefore begin with their effect on the liar, rather than with their consequences in the outside world. Lying
brings about a rupture between the speaker and God by corrupting the gift of
language by which we are able to cultivate our inner selves, express our inner-
most thoughts and feelings, understand each other, and speak the truth, which is
how human beings connect with God. Lies are the antimatter of truth, disinte-
grating the medium of language through which God can make his presence felt
on earth.

One of the few later writers to embrace Augustine's absolutist approach to
lying was Dante, who invented the eighth circle of his hell for liars. Murderers
only made it to the seventh circle of Dante's Hell; the ninth circle was reserved
for traitors, who can be viewed as a species of liar who combines lying with the
active betrayal of a benefactor. Yet most modern writers and thinkers who are
not actively recruiting for some religious organization or another nowadays
would feel inwardly squeamish at the idea of endorsing even the rather mild ob-
jections to lying put forward by Aristotle. Most modern people believe that lying
is a normal human activity and that we would be hard-pressed to get through the
day without telling at least one lie, the consequences of which are often prefer-
able to those of telling the truth.

One proof that is often given of the universality of lying is a possibly apoc-
ryphal story about Koko the gorilla, who famously learned over one thousand
hand signs taught to her by scientists at Stanford University, and was said to
understand over two thousand words of spoken English. After ripping a steel
sink from its moorings inside her cage, Koko was said to have blamed the damage on one of her pet cats. We smile at this story because we are the children
of Machiavelli and Nietzsche rather than Augustine. Rather than believing that
the world is a reservoir of truth available to us through language, we are more

ity of liars who grease the wheels of commerce, love, sex, and all other activities in which mankind engages. Adam and Eve lied to God and to each other. "The check is in the mail" is always a lie, just as "I love you" is only a partial version of the whole truth. Men and women lie with the justifiable assurance that the lies they tell are variations of the same lies that have been told by their slippery ancestors since the beginning of time. We cheat, conceal, contrive, counterfeit, deceive, defraud, dissemble, exaggerate, fabricate, fake, feign, impersonate, lie, misinform, misrepresent, pretend, and prevaricate. In most times and places there is also a floating population of those who are lost in illusions of their own making and might see themselves as embarking on a great adventure, but are simply lost.

---

apt to believe that the truth is hidden from us and that language is a lie. Starting from a position of doubt, we struggle to get in contact with a reality that often eludes us.

VI. On the Run

Making a neat picture out of the mixed-up puzzle pieces of who James Hogue was and who he claimed to be is a professional challenge that paled next to the mystery of what he was actually trying to do with his life over the twenty years that his path had intersected here and there with mine. The idea that his life was a mirror in which other people might see themselves more clearly was a myth that he encouraged and perpetuated in order to blind people to his ends. Still, it was hard not to see his story as a kind of *Pilgrim's Progress* in reverse, a cracked reflection of a life story that was shared in some way by his classmates at Princeton and with the lives of tens of thousands of other graduates of Ivy League colleges and ski-poster towns. In his story of isolation and imposture it might be possible to glimpse something that might not be ordinarily visible about the generic life that was shared by a particular group of people in a very particular moment in time.

What made his activity so baffling to those who studied it up close was the absence of the spectacular payoff that one would expect from a stylish Hollywood movie—the stolen Matisse in his coat closet, the speedboat sheltering in a cove on the French Riviera, a bag of diamonds gone missing from a vault in London, the secret bank account in Switzerland. Hogue's copper pots, his five sets of skis, and the stolen moose head hardly qualified him as a cinematic criminal. He was more like the hayseed Jay Gatz than the urbane young criminal who became Jay Gatsby. His seeming lack of ambition, his soft-spoken nature, and his habit of giving gifts led some people who knew him to insist that he wasn't a criminal at all, and that he was instead an innocent person who went about things in the wrong way. His defenders correctly pointed out that Hogue showed no actual tendencies towards physical violence, although he did leave behind a record of threatening phone calls to women who in one way or another had displeased him, including a shy, crippled violin student in Aspen, who played me the angry messages that he left on her answering machine.

Yet the portrait of Hogue as a gentle, misunderstood loser is belied by the length of his criminal career and his lack of remorse for his crimes, which included offenses against property and institutions that destroyed the fabric of trust that binds people to each other. His goal was not money or diamonds or twenty-four-karat gold watches. He wanted to make other people's lives his own. To say that Hogue was smart enough to have acquired university degrees or a house in Telluride by legal means misses the point of acquiring these particular trophies in the way that he did. He stole because he was a thief, a role that allowed him to move in circles into which he might not have otherwise been accepted while exposing the hollowness of the distinctions and accomplishments that adhere to the privileged status of others. Fraud provided him with a sense of superiority that was essential to his feeling of well-being. His story was a throwback to a time when masquerades of race and gender and class were more practical in some ways than they are in our information-glutted age, when an officer in the Mountain Village police department could gain access to chapters of Hogue's life simply by typing "James Hogue" into Google. Yet there is also a sense in which Hogue's singular quest, the way he went about his business, was itself a product of the information age. He was a hacker, for whom finding a shortcut through the thicket of requirements and pathways laid down by the operation of large systems was a life-affirming challenge that lessened his sense of isolation and provided him with a sense of purpose at the same time as it condemned him to a life that was impossible to share or sustain.

• • •

James Hogue was arrested on February 4, 2006, while surfing the World Wide Web on a stolen laptop at the Barnes & Noble at the Foothills Mall in Tucson, Arizona. It was Saturday afternoon, and Hogue was spotted by an employee of the large bookstore chain who recognized the skinny fugitive from a wanted poster that was hanging near the employee lounge. Hogue had been under surveillance by federal marshals who had tracked his movements through Oro Valley and Oracle, Arizona, northeast of Tucson, where he had been staying at a rural compound owned by the Salentre family of New Jersey.

According to law enforcement and organized crime sources in New Jersey, the Salentre family's involvement in illegal activities centered around the trafficking of stolen goods in New Jersey, Arizona, Colorado, and elsewhere. Donald Salentre Jr. had been Hogue's cell mate in a New Jersey prison where Hogue did time for his most celebrated fraud; Salentre Jr. had been sentenced for receiving stolen property. The marshals flew a helicopter over the Salentre compound and spotted Hogue's truck, the license plates of which had been switched with the plates of a truck that belonged to Donald Salentre Jr.

When he was caught in the Barnes & Noble, Hogue had $1,200 in cash and appeared to be preparing for a new life as doctor, with CD-ROMs on anatomy, clinical consultation, and the principles of internal medicine. He was arrested and brought to the Pima County Jail, where his first phone calls were to the Salentre family home in Trenton. Hogue contacted the Salentres soon after leaving Telluride. The tapes of his phone calls show Hogue as a family friend of career criminals who provided him with money, lawyers, and other resources while he was on the run.

"They caught me," Hogue announced. He asked if a family friend named Jeff would pick up his truck at the mall where he had been arrested.

"Are you guys gonna bail me out?" he asked. Bail was set at $120,000. If he couldn't make bail, Hogue threatened to do something drastic. "I'm just gonna hang it up," he said. While it sounded like a threat to kill himself, it was also clearly a message that he was feeling desperate. He would do anything, including flip on the Salentre family, in order to avoid doing time. Even five days in jail would be too much, Hogue suggested.

"I did eight and a half years!" the criminal on the other end of the phone laughed.

"Fuck, man. I'm really, really depressed," Hogue said. He wanted the Salentres to get money from his bank account in New York and send it to his fiancée, Irina, in Russia. In a second phone call to the Salentre family he talked directly to his old cell mate.

"Somebody could kill eighty people and not get this bullshit," Hogue fumed. "I mean, shit, there's no way out of this." He wanted Jack, the Salentre family bagman, to come out to Colorado and arrange for his assets to be transferred to Irina. "If I can't get out of this, I'm gonna hang it up," he said. "That's why I need Jack to come down here, you know. Tell him it's desperate."

When the family got hold of Jack, however, it turned out that the bank account had been frozen. Hogue then turned to his nephew, Brian Patrick, the person he was closest to in his extended family. While Jim became a scam artist and an impostor, Patrick was studying community ecology, a branch of biology; he specialized in beetles and spiders. With his inquiring mind and prankish disposition, Patrick offered a plausible version of the life that Hogue might have led if going straight had been an option. Their exchange revealed some of the family weirdness that had helped to shape Jim, as well as some of the plans that had been interrupted by his arrest in Tucson.

"So you got caught, eh?" Patrick asked. "Hanging out at the Barnes & Noble?"

"Yeah," Jim admitted.

Patrick laughed. "I expected you'd be a little more sneaky, Jim." Hogue allowed that he hadn't been sneaky enough.

"I heard you tried to call Grandma," Patrick said. Hogue said that he had tried to call his mother, but that he hadn't been able to get through. "You know Grandma, you called collect and she wasn't gonna take those charges," Patrick snorted. "So let's cut to the chase here. Are you calling for something, or are you just calling to say hi?"

When Hogue didn't answer, Patrick tried a different tack. "Did you hear Betty died?" he asked, referring to Hogue's full sister. Jim had heard the news.

"You know I've been going over to Russia, and I have a fiancée over there," he added. What he wanted was for his nephew to call Irina and tell her that he had been killed in a car crash. Patrick tended in practice to emulate the behavior of his father's straight-arrow parents, and was not enthusiastic about lying to his uncle's fiancée—a real person, whom Hogue met on a trip he took to Russia with a few other men from Telluride, who had joined together for the purpose of finding wives. "Well, this might be one of the better times to come clean," Patrick suggested.

"I don't know how long I'm gonna be here, and I just can't keep her tied up like that," Hogue objected. "You get where I'm coming from, right? It's kind of a moral dilemma." When Patrick suggested that his fiancée might show up to the funeral or want to visit Hogue's grave, his uncle showed that he had thought things through. "No, she can't get a visa," he said. Then he lowered the ante.

"Well how about a coma?" he asked hopefully.

Patrick laughed. "A Google search on you comes up now like you wouldn't believe," he said.

"Yeah. I understand," Hogue answered.

Unwilling to give up on his fantasy, Hogue then called Salentre back. "I'm gonna have to have somebody tell her I died in a car crash, or I'm in a coma or something," he said, hoping to convince his old cell mate to call Irina.

"Tell her you're being detained right now," his ex-cell mate dryly suggested.

"No, no, no. That never works."

"She'll write you letters then," Salentre teased. "I'm not gonna tell her you died," he said. "I'll tell her that you won't be seeing her for a while."

"That's worse than anything," Hogue objected. Salentre's patience was wearing thin.

"Where'd you find her, in a mail-order catalogue?" he asked. Hogue answered that he had met her in Russia at a party.

"Oh, yeah?" Salentre asked. "Well, that's the least of your problems right now."

"Damn, I wish Jack would get here and get those credit cards, start running them up, maxing them out," Hogue said. But the opportunity to run up bad debts on his personal credit cards was long since past. A few days later, he was flown back to Telluride in a sleek private jet belonging to the governor of the state of Colorado. Except for the fact that he was shackled and handcuffed, and dressed in an orange prison shirt, the flight was exactly as Jim might have imagined it. The beard he had grown in jail was neatly trimmed for the flight. He never said a word, preferring to keep what remained of his tattered mystery intact. Once or twice, he took a few sips from a bottle of Nestlé water. For most of the flight, he pretended to sleep, occasionally peeking out at his captors.

Allergic to penicillin, the fugitive Donald Eugene Webb is a lover of dogs, a flashy dresser, and a big tipper. I first encountered Webb, a darkly handsome fellow with deep-set eyes and a prominent forehead, on the FBI's Ten Most Wanted Poster, a relic from the days of John Dillinger and Bonnie and Clyde, which I read from top to bottom while hanging around the entrance to the Mountain Village police department. Described as "a career criminal and master of assumed identities," Webb is being sought by the FBI in connection with the murder of a police chief. He specializes in robbing jewelry stores. Killing the police chief in the course of a robbery was probably a mistake, I thought. As of this writing, Webb has been on the FBI's Ten Most Wanted list for over twenty-five years without being caught. I can't help but wonder whether Donald Eugene Webb is someone you might become by accident.

My reverie was interrupted by Robert Walraven, a big, crew-cut Texan wearing a blue denim shirt, blue jeans, and a green fleece jacket. The detective who pursued Hogue to Arizona, Walraven has the broad shoulders and blunt manners of a Texas football coach. A certificate from the "National Institute for Truth Verification" pronounces him a "Certified Fraud Examiner." He tells me that Jim is a career criminal who is not sorry for what he has done and is unlikely to ever change.

"Honestly, somebody needs to know where he is at all times just like you track a sex offender, because if he's in your community, a crime's likely being committed," Walraven said. What he told me about Jim is a version of a theory that has dominated police work in America for the last sixty years, which rests in large part on a fascinating and quietly hilarious book that I have been reading off and on late at night in the room that I have rented in Telluride. It is no knock on Robert Walraven or other hardworking practitioners of the fine art of criminal justice to note that few working police officers have heard of *The Mask of Sanity* or of its author, Hervey Cleckley, a name whose clattering syllables sit uneasily in any normal sentence, just as Cleckley's subjects—psychopaths—have trouble fitting in to human society. While Hervey Cleckley never attained the widespread fame of contemporaries like Karl Menninger, his influence on the use of applied psychology in the American legal system has arguably been greater than that of anyone besides Freud. It is to Cleckley that judges, lawyers, and pulp-fiction writers alike owe our fondness for psychopaths and sociopaths, those lone rangers of the psyche whose existence on a plane outside normal conceptions of good and evil is an affront to more ecumenical notions of a shared morality.

Written in courtly, antique prose, Cleckley's book is a fascinating and highly entertaining collection of firsthand accounts of the author's experiences working with deeply recalcitrant and incorrigible patients in asylums and hospitals in the American South, particularly in the state of Georgia. Through these case histories, Cleckley distinguishes a population of "forgotten" human beings, intelligent and not suffering from any of the classical psychological disorders, who nonetheless fail to demonstrate any noticeable adherence to the moral codes by which the rest of mankind ostensibly chooses to live. One subject was a habitual drunkard and screwup. Another man, whose name is given as Stanley, induced five teenage girls to shave their heads for no apparent reason. Absent any natural inclination to abide by the law, or to feel guilty when violating even the most basic codes of human behavior, Cleckley wrote, this population lived a separate existence of its own, like a tribe of space aliens among the run of more or less normal or abnormal human beings, who are regularly beset by conformity and guilt:

> It becomes difficult to imagine how much of the sham and hollowness which cynical commentators have immemorially pointed out in life may come from contact in serious issues with persons affected in some serious degree by the disorder we are trying to describe. The fake poet who really feels little; the painter who, de-

spite his loftiness, had his eye chiefly on the lucrative fad of his day; the fashionable clergyman who, despite his burning eloquence or his lively castigation of the devil, is primarily concerned with his advancement; the flirt who can readily awaken love but cannot feel love or recognize its absence; parents who, despite smooth convictions that they have only the child's welfare at heart, actually reject him except as it suits their own petty or selfish aims. . . .

Sanity, the outward show of understanding and adhering to social norms, was a mask that these exiles from a shared humanity could put on when necessary, and throw off when feeling loony, unsettled, or bored. The price of this masquerade was a deep loneliness and an inability to make meaningful and fulfilling contact with others. While the absence of guilt made it possible for Cleckley's sociopaths to deceive others with ease, the lack of a shared connection with normal human emotion made it difficult for the sociopath to sustain his masquerade for long periods of time. Sooner or later, his shallow acquaintance with socially connected emotions like guilt, love, and loss would land him in jail or a mental hospital.

Part of the pleasure of reading Cleckley is that sociopaths, and psychopaths, really do exist. The other pleasure of reading Cleckley is that the joke is as often on us as it is on them. The longer you think about Cleckley's case histories, the harder it gets to keep friends and co-workers and spouses off the list. Published in 1941, as the world teetered on the brink of madness, Cleckley's book was less the product of a strict scientific methodology than a kind of inspired backwater guess about the strictly conventional nature of social behavior that would become commonplace after the war in the work of hipster urban sociologists like Erving Goffman, for whom all social behavior might be profitably analyzed using the model of the relationship between the con man and his mark.

I asked Walraven if he thinks that Hogue might have used his education to do some good in the world if Princeton University hadn't thrown him out before he graduated.

"I don't think it would have been as simple as, 'I'm gonna get a house with a white picket fence,' " he said. "He'd have been one of those involved in one of those other big frauds, whether it be Enron or something else." The reason criminals like Hogue get caught, he said, is not because police officers are so dogged in their investigations, but because the criminals are unable to stop. "I've seen people get away with stuff for five years that are committing fraud and embezzlement, and then they get too comfortable," he said. "This morning I was listening on the radio to a guy who had won the three-hundred-million dollar lottery, Jack whatever his name is. You know, he ain't got a penny left, and he's still writing bad checks. He had a hundred and ten million dollars that he wasted." Behind him were boxes filled with papers and three large binders of photographs and stolen property reports related to Hogue that Walraven occasionally consults as we speak in order to refresh his mind about the details of particular cases.

Walraven estimates that Hogue stole over seven thousand items worth over $100,000. I asked the detective why he is pursuing Hogue for an admittedly huge accumulation of essentially victimless crimes—where no one was hurt in any lasting way, where insurance companies generally covered the losses, and even Hogue appeared to be baffled as to how he might benefit directly from his actions. Because Telluride is a resort town, he answered, property crimes pose a direct threat to the local economy. People whose homes are invaded and whose possessions are stolen lose their accustomed sense of safety and protection.

Their sense of connection to their neighbors and to the larger community is strained. They feel violated.

"You take the old couple from Kansas City that he burglarized on one occasion—a thirty-thousand-dollar-plus property loss," he said, sounding entirely sincere. "You sit down and talk to that couple, and they don't feel safe in their home anymore. That antique rocking horse meant a lot to them. Now they're getting it back."

When Hogue was captured by the federal marshals in Arizona, Walraven flew down to Tucson and interviewed the captive in jail. A tape of the interview shows a determined investigator who had studied the case with care. Still, his quarry continued to elude him.

"Do you have any interest in telling me where the rest of the property is that I haven't found?" Walraven asked.

Hogue played dumb.

"I don't know what it is. Do you have a list?" he asked, accusing Walraven of making vague accusations.

"No, I'm not," Walraven defended himself. "In 2003, there's an antique rocking horse, leather chair, and paintings, hand-woven rugs. I'm not being vague when I describe a big rocking horse by your front door. The leather chair that was in your living room. That's not vague. They were in your house." The list of items made the detective sound silly.

"Where are they now?" Hogue asked.

"They're in evidence."

"Well," Hogue answered, "then why are you asking me about them?"

Walraven paused, and then regained his bearings. "You told me on January 4 you're building a house. Remember that?" he asked.

"I remember passing your lie detector test," Hogue said, referring to a test to which he had voluntarily submitted to in Telluride before he left town. "I remember that much."

Walraven made his annoyance clear. The test showed that Hogue always told the truth, he said angrily, even on the control questions that he was supposed to lie about, like the color of the wall in front of him. "What does that mean?" he asked Hogue.

"I don't know. You're the one who was saying you're the expert," Hogue answered. Sullen at the beginning of the interview, he was clearly enjoying himself. "Well I think that, uh, your office is a little overstaffed," he added. He also expressed his dissatisfaction with a documentary film about his life that had appeared in 2002. Called *Con Man*, the film was produced by a filmmaker named Jesse Moss, who came to me for help after reading an article I wrote about Hogue in 1995 for the *Washington Post*.

"You sounded like a pretty good track star," Walraven offered.

"Not really," Hogue answered, modestly. "I was seventeen years old, running against people that were Kenyan Olympians. I mean, I didn't expect to be able to beat them."

When it came to the question of the stolen goods he had dumped out by Trout Lake, near the old water tower, he was no more forthcoming.

"You talking about the water tower on the road? Near the entrance to Trout Lake?" Hogue asked. "I don't know anything about that water tower. I think you got your locations mixed up."

"I don't think you could tell the truth if you had to," Walraven said.

"I don't think you know what you're talking about," Hogue answered.

"I think I do," Walraven said.

"Well, I know you don't," Hogue said.

"How do you know I don't?" Walraven asked.

"Well first of all, I don't know anything about the water tower," Hogue answered, adding, "I know where the water tower is."

When Walraven accused him of being a liar, he showed his disdain for the word by shrugging his shoulders. "I would think that one lie would make a person a liar," he answered. "Going by that makes you a liar, because you've lied to me at least once."

"What did I lie about?" Walraven asked.

"Oh, I can't remember now," Hogue answered airily. "But I remember thinking, 'Oh, that was a lie.'"

VII. The Sentence

In a series of letters that he wrote from jail in Colorado to Brian Patrick, Hogue arranged for money to be transferred to his fiancée. He also tried to negotiate a plea deal with the state using Patrick as a go-between. Details of his business affairs were mixed with breezy accounts of his adventures in the sciences that present themselves as the writings of a devoted naturalist with a broad and eccentric field of knowledge and a large library at his disposal. Perusing Hogue's learned entomological correspondence, it comes as a shock to remember that the author is a drifter who is sitting in jail.

"It seems that you are doing an awful lot of taxonomy, and that distinction is still as important as it was thirty years ago when I was working with Lepidoptera," Hogue wrote. In his day, he continued, "We all thought that the great new thing was electrophoresis gels to separate proteins; sort of a primitive DNA analysis." While there is something giggle-inducing about watching Hogue try to game his cousin (his experience with "Lepidoptera" was a summer he spent collecting butterflies in Wyoming in 1977), he was also capable of referring to the somewhat dated but fascinating works of the naturalist Alexander Petrunkevitch, author of *An Inquiry into the Natural Classification of Spiders*, a subject which happened to be his nephew's primary area of academic interest.

How and when the work of the late Yale professor, a Russian émigré and contemporary of Nabokov, had attracted Hogue's attention was not clear. But it wasn't hard to see what in Petrunkevitch's work had caught his interest. "I remember reading his really good essay about how the bigger wasps g. *pepsis* prey upon tarantulas," Hogue wrote, citing an old issue of *Scientific American* from the 1950s in which he believed the article had appeared.

"If the wasp attacked the wrong species, it lost, but it never lost against the correct species," he wrote, clearly fascinated by the way that giant wasps could defeat the poisonous spiders by biting them in a specific place in their midsections where they were most vulnerable. "There was probably some chemical identifier for the wasps and maybe some chemical means for the wasp to mollify the spider," he speculated. Nature was a game, in which animals were always searching for an advantage over others. The techniques of the game interested him the way they would interest any naturalist.

When he appeared in court for sentencing in front of Judge James Schum, Hogue looked nothing like the lean athlete who could run twenty miles in a day and pass for ten or fifteen years younger than he was. Appearing gaunt and disheveled in the courtroom, he seemed to be sick, an effect that he accentuated by growing his hair and beard long. He sat in the courtroom and listened impassively to his criminal history, which by now included ten arrests and seven convictions for fraud, forged checks, impersonation, trespassing, and larceny. The court also heard that he had been rejected by seven or eight community correction facilities but accepted by a program in San Luis Valley that would allow him to serve out his sentence in a supervised community setting.

Hogue's attorney, Harvey Palefsky, was unable to find anyone in the state of Colorado who would agree to testify on his client's behalf. When he saw Cindy Putnam at his client's sentencing hearing, he instructed Judge Schum to call her to the stand. Having had no prior indication that she would be asked to speak, the witness stammered, then froze like a frightened deer. Later, Putnam wished that she had been able to stand up in the courtroom and say a few positive things about her old running partner. She had great empathy for Hogue, who was a human being not unlike herself—a shy person who tried to avoid hurting others, and whose motives were generally pure. He might benefit from the kind of help that a good psychiatrist might be able to provide. But her native shyness, her lack of preparation, the unexpected pressure of the moment, and her doubts about the true parameters of Hogue's deceptive nature made it impossible for Putnam to say even a single word. The only person left to speak before the judge and the assembled spectators was James Hogue.

"I would have pled guilty last year, but I was trying to get whatever I could back to my family," he explained to Judge Schum. "In the last month or so, I've been able to do that, and give away whatever property I have."

Schum appeared frustrated by Hogue's unwillingness or inability to take responsibility for his crimes.

"I've stolen some things, and I've also purchased some things that [might have been] stolen," Hogue finally answered. "It's hard to explain why." He told the judge that he might be suffering from "some sort of collection compulsion," which might in turn explain why he never disposed of all the property in his house. The judge was not impressed.

"Well, you have a collection compulsion," he said. "Do you collect anything besides stolen items? Like rocks, books, or bottles?"

"Rocks?" Hogue asked, surprised. The question of rocks was a tricky one. A further search into the defendant's criminal record would have revealed that he had stolen a quantity of precious gems and minerals from Harvard University. "Um, books," he decided. "Classical CDs."

"That wasn't enough to satisfy the compulsion?" the judge asked, in a way that didn't sound friendly.

"I guess not," Hogue answered. When Schum asked Hogue

about his discussion of running up debts on his credit card, Hogue's answer was not convincing.

"Well actually, it was not credit cards I was talking about," he said, despite clear evidence to the contrary on the taped phone call that had just been played in the courtroom. "I have ATMs that go to my bank account. I don't see why I can't use my ATM." Hogue may have also been pretending to seem weak-minded and pathetic in order to buy a reduction in his sentence, and the strategy showed some signs of working. "It seems to me that there's almost a mental health issue," Judge Schum speculated out loud to the courtroom. While it might have been better for Hogue to take Brian Patrick's advice and come clean to Irina, his attempted deception of his fiancée was hardly a crime. The true nature of Hogue's problem was not hard to diagnose.

"You have a long history of ripping people off," he said. "It goes back to 1983. And part of the problem here is that you just don't seem to learn the lesson through these various lighter sentences that you've received over the years." Over the course of more than two decades, Hogue's history of theft had escalated from bad checks for a few hundred dollars to thefts of property worth thousands of dollars. "And it's getting more serious," Judge Schum said, as he anatomized Hogue's criminal progress, "because you are breaking into homes."

Hogue was a menace not only to private property but to the feeling of security that made it possible for Telluride to function as a high-end resort town. He was a bad neighbor. "You're giving your own neighbors a line about how you're gonna be the good guy and look out for them, and then you're turning around and ripping them off behind their backs," Judge Schum concluded. He sentenced James Hogue to the maximum term of ten years in a state penitentiary.

Hogue's attorney called the sentence "a waste of talent and

brainpower." It was hard to imagine that anyone in the court-room that day would have disagreed with the statement. At the same time, it was hard to fault the people of Telluride for no longer wanting Hogue around.

Cindy Putnam visited Hogue in jail one last time to express her regrets for freezing up in the courtroom. Hogue apologized for putting her on the spot. Her testimony wouldn't have made any difference anyway, he said. The judge didn't care about the facts of the case, or who James Hogue really was. He had made up his mind prior to the hearing.

After Hogue was moved to the state prison in Canon City, Putnam heard from him once more. He spent from six in the morning until ten at night outside, he wrote. He hiked twenty miles a day and did some jogging too, which was difficult because of his work boots. He no longer complained of feeling sick or having tumors, the way he did when he was in jail in San Marcos. He sounded confident and strong. He asked Putnam to send him money for running shoes, clothes, and a radio, so he could listen to NPR.

Hogue had given Putnam title to his white Toyota truck before his sentencing hearing in May, a fact that might have influenced her testimony on his behalf, had she offered it in court. Having declined to testify, she was more than happy to wire him some part of the cash value of his truck. She wrote him several letters to make sure that he had received the money, but he never wrote back or called. Perhaps a bond of trust had been broken by Putnam's failure to speak on his behalf in court after he gave her his truck, or perhaps maintaining contact with people outside was too much of a strain. Perhaps she was starting to know him too well. Dick Unruh, a local attorney who had helped plot Hogue's legal strategy, also tried to contact Hogue to see if he was okay, but he never wrote back or called him, either. No one I spoke to in Telluride ever heard from Hogue again.

VIII. Visiting Day

On a clear and cold winter afternoon towards the end of my stay, I went to visit James Hogue in San Miguel County jail in Ilium. Aside from the residents of the nearby ski condos, no one really lives in Ilium, which is about ten miles down the road from the mining town of Placerville. The San Miguel County jail sits at the end of a service road in the shade of three ten-thousand-foot-high mountains. Plenty of Telluride residents have spent a night or two here for driving drunk. Aside from a navy Plymouth Valiant, a later model of the family car that my parents used to drive, and a half-dozen trucks from the sheriff's department, the parking lot was empty. Outside the entrance to the jail were three slender young aspens, like the trees in Hogue's backyard. It would be hard to imagine a more beautiful spot for a jail.

Despite my previous failed attempts to see Jim, I felt sure he would see me this time, if only because he didn't have many visitors. "He doesn't see many people," the jail clerk agreed, as she read over my latest application. With his taste for spectacular surroundings, it made sense that Hogue would wind up in a jail at the top of the Rockies, looking out on snow-capped peaks and high tree lines that could equal anything supplied by his imaginative universe, in which other human beings play only minor roles. After mentioning the natural beauty of the setting, I asked the clerk, an older woman in a county uniform, if inmates could see the mountains from their cells.

"They can't see anything," the clerk answered, matter-of-factly. When I took her answer to mean that the cells looked out over the parking lot, she corrected me again. The windows of the cells faced a concrete wall and were made of unbreakable

translucent glass that let in light but no other visual data that
might stimulate the prisoners.

The clerk on duty agreed to take a letter to Hogue, in which I
suggested that we had a lot to talk about, that I could send him
books, that there might be money for a film about his life, and
whatever other inducements I could think of that might encourage an isolated man to talk to me about the enigmatic roots of his
life. I had never cooperated with the law enforcement officials
who wanted to put him away. On the other hand, I didn't think
that he was innocent of the crimes with which he was charged. I
looked at his case the way a biologist might. James Hogue was another animal in the forest. His behavior interested me, because
each and every life is connected to each and every other life. By
understanding Jim's life, I might reach a more detailed and com-
prehensive understanding of the ecology of a forest that shelters
many different kinds of life whose awareness of each other is
only partial. Because we are social animals, we are vulnerable to
impostors, who tell us what we want to hear, and who trade the
simple pleasures of human companionship for more abstract
pleasures that cannot be shared with others. I would also come to
a better understanding of why lying is wrong, and not simply a
normal part of everyday human behavior.

Back in my room, I sat on the bed with a notebook on my lap
open to a fresh page with the name "James Hogue" underscored
twice for added emphasis. I tried to think of something clever to
write. He was too abstract to be a good thief. Maybe he liked
being alone in his mountain cell, watching the light outside his
room get brighter and then darker. Maybe he was watching the
Chargers-Patriots game on TV.

The question of how writers come to appropriate the lives of
the people they write about is a tricky one. The morally upright
stance is that writers tell the truth and that everyone else in the
universe exists at their pleasure, to provide them with quotations

and documents. The false humility that so many writers show in the face of the lived experience of their subjects is belied by the act of writing, which always involves a head-on collision between someone else's actual life and the writer's inner life. While it is facile to equate journalism with lying, it is also true that both actions share in common an unpleasantly instrumental approach to people and to language that diminishes the common store of trust. The subject has no power to alter a reporter's approach to his or her subject, or to take back a single word that they said. I waited for another hour but Hogue still didn't call.

The next day, I sat on my bed at the appointed time and the phone rang, but I didn't answer it. Instead, through a mutual friend, I sent Hogue another letter. This time, I received an envelope containing a handwritten response written in No. 2 pencil on four sheets of blue-lined white paper.

"Thank you for your very nice letter," the familiar voice began. He couldn't see a good book coming out of his story, he said, because there would be too many gaps; "the good stuff" would be missing. The residue of peevishness or boredom in his answers was most likely the product of the fact that he was in jail. It was the voice of a man who was trapped in a situation that he had created, and which had deprived him of his accustomed ability to take control.

"You became a liar when you told that first lie as a child in the same way a murderer becomes a murderer with their first murder," he wrote, in response to a question I asked him about whether he had ever felt deceived in our interactions. He could not have felt deceived, he wrote, because he had never believed a single word I said to him.

"Do you miss the mountains?" I had wondered.

"No."

"What do you imagine during the day?"

"Not Much."

"How do you keep your mind occupied during the day?"

"Sleep."

Telluride was worse than Princeton, he wrote. "Here is unbridled greed. There is maybe not as shallow. You've been to both; don't ask me!"

He was not planning to become a doctor in Russia, as the CD-ROMs and the books about anatomy had seemed to suggest. He claimed not to understand my questions about wanting to become a fictional character, or whether there was any such thing as "the real you."

"If you could be James Hogue in high school in Kansas, or Alexi Santana at Princeton, or Jim Hogue in Telluride, or any of your other former selves, right now, who would you be and why?" I asked him.

"I don't know, maybe there are more choices?" he answered. Having done his assigned writing for the day, he turned the tables.

"Now, for your questions," he began.

1. Are you greatly dismayed by the sum of your life?

2. Is your mother proud of you?

3. Despite having an abundance of personal charisma and imagination, Hunter Thompson was only partially able to impose himself into others' stories. Do you feel that this is a good strategy for you, as a lesser light? Do you ever want to have your own story?

4. Does the success of Uzodinma Iweala annoy you? Do you feel you should have had that talent and luck bestowed upon you?

I looked Uzodinma Iweala up on Google, and was impressed by the young Nigerian novelist's achievements. By that point, the insult had gone flat. Envy was a major theme of his insults. He wondered if I envied the achievements of the writers on the *Harvard Lampoon* who went on to write for *The Simpsons*.

5. Did you ever feel a great sense of entitlement? If so, why? Do you now?

The privileges I enjoy by having graduated from Harvard and Princeton are silly. I like *The Simpsons*, especially the pictures, which are produced by teams of skilled animators who work in a complex outside of Seoul, South Korea, a nearly first-world nation which lives under constant threat from the Hermit Kingdom of the North. When I try to imagine the life of my Korean counterpart, I see an overly serious corporate servant with straight black hair and a good degree and nothing to eat in her refrigerator aside from a single container of blueberry yogurt.

As I watched the news on TV that night, I learned that Malibu was burning; it had been the lead story on the evening news for three nights in a row. The chaparral is natural fuel that leaves oils behind in the ground when it burns; after it rains, the mud slides off the hills like grease from a frying pan. The homes of a multiplatinum singer and an Oscar-winning director were gone, as was the residence of a local cartoonist whose multimillion-dollar spread featured sliding glass doors opening onto a redwood deck cantilevered over Carbon Canyon, a sheer, two-hundred-and-sixty-foot drop to the Pacific. Sixty-three houses, each worth more than a million dollars a piece, had gone up in smoke. The fire raced six hundred feet in thirty seconds, devouring everything in its path, popping cedar-shingled roofs and raining firebrands down on the beach where I once swam and tried to surf. I saw news footage of the helicopters hosing down the slopes and lumbering seaplanes that swooped down out of the sky and dumped ocean water on the flames. When I lived in Los Angeles I once tried to write a cartoon show called *I.Q. Jones* about a sprightly subatomic particle who was black, heavily into physics, and bore a strong physical resemblance to one of the less fortunate California Raisins. I thank God that *I.Q. Jones* never made it onto the air. I felt bad for James Hogue. His chance at recovering some grip on a normal life had slid through his fingers here. The wreckage was plain and affecting, even if he was also an asshole.

James Hogue hated anything associated with being ordinary, the same way that I did. He just went about things in a different way. The final question he posed in his letter sounded entirely sincere.

"6. What is it with the janitor's clothing?" he wrote, wondering about my preference for army surplus jackets and worn blue jeans. "Was or is it a statement of solidarity with the lumpen?"

"Ciao," he wrote, without signing his name.

IX. SuperStar

In a local café, I met a girl named SuperStar. She had been Hogue's girlfriend in town before he went to Russia and met the blonde doctor, and pretended again to be someone new. Super-Star was the name she used in our conversations on the Internet. She had black dyed hair and a necklace. I found her because of a notation in the prison record made by a local clergyman who put $25 on Hogue's commissary account. We began a correspondence, and she finally agreed to have coffee with me.

Jim would always have a book with him, she remembered, and he grew good weed. All her friends bought weed from Jim. That was a new part of the story. He said he was twenty-eight years old. She thought that was funny, since he was obviously older: he was probably in his thirties. She was eighteen. They met hanging out on the slopes, and he kept asking her out to dinner. Jim used to come over and visit her at her house.

When he was with SuperStar, Jim talked all the time. He would talk about art. He would talk about random things he read in books. SuperStar was impressed because he was different than the local eighteen- and twenty-year-olds who got high on the slopes.

"We were together a lot," she said. "Sometimes he wouldn't come over until one in the morning, because I was working." Barely out of high school, she had already learned to make allowances for any man who might show her a little bit of attention. Kind, bright, but unsure of herself, she is overweight, and dyes her hair black. It might be easy to make her feel unloved.

"He was a very shy person," SuperStar remembered, looking over at her friend, whom she had brought with her to the café for protection. Her friend is so pretty that it is hard not to stare. SuperStar will never steal her pretty friend's boyfriends. SuperStar and her friend exist on different planes of existence, looks-wise. One is ethereal, gorgeous, a vision of college sophomore loveliness in soft sweatpants and a tight sweater able to make the heart of any man beat faster. The other is a sullen, earth-bound girl, garishly painted. Jim took care of himself. He took care of SuperStar. They would talk two or three times a day on the phone.

When I asked her for personal details about her lover, she mentions how much he loved Christmas. "He had a huge collection of Christmas music. He loved any type of Christmas song." It was rare to meet an adult who was in love with Christmas in such an unreserved and uncynical way. "He said that he had a mother," she remembered. "I never got into the family stuff because it was a touchy subject for him." She was his family.

SuperStar was the one visitor that Hogue's neighbors remember ever coming to his house on San Bernardo. Downstairs was his wood shop, she remembers. Hogue heated the upstairs with a wood stove. In the living room he kept a wooden carousel horse. Hogue was eager to impress the young girl by telling her about the books he had read and showing off his skills at cooking and woodworking. "He'd tell me he was really smart," she recalled. He would cook for her, and they'd watch movies together. He especially enjoyed watching movies about New York, she remembered. He also liked watching movies in Russian.

SuperStar liked being with him enough that she stopped smoking pot. Soon she noticed that he stayed up late and had long conversations on the phone in Russian. She felt like she might be going crazy. Up late one night, she aimlessly entered his name into the Google search engine. She learned that there were parts of Hogue's past he hadn't told her about, including the fact that he had spent time in jail. She confronted her boyfriend, who at first insisted that he was not the person she had read about on-line. "It's my cousin who looks like me," he said. SuperStar didn't believe him. "I thought I would come here and get away," he said. Then he broke down and cried. Before that, "I'd never seen him sad or upset," SuperStar remembered.

She stayed with him because she wanted to help him, she said, sounding like any other woman who stays with a man because she wants to save him. Maybe he would change. Maybe he would finally tell her the truth about his past. When he finally left town, she felt relieved, but she was worried for him, too. She called his cell phone when he was on the run, and he took her calls.

"Have you gone crazy?" she asked him.

"I guess I have," he answered. She thinks he told her that he loved her, but she is not sure. The story is at once pathetic and touching, because it shows what nearly all of us will do to hear the reassuring voice on the other end of the phone. Next to the promise of love, very little else matters. The next morning she found his jacket in her car with a note that said, "Happy belated Christmas, I love you, James." He stayed in town for at least two weeks after he disappeared, living in abandoned condos, to see if things would cool down, and planning his getaway to Arizona, where he would start a new life.

When I asked SuperStar for a positive memory of being with Jim, she remembers spending time with him outdoors. "He loved being out in the snow, or in the mountains in the summer," she remembered. He also loved kids, or the idea of kids, and spoke about having children. "But he can't have kids," SuperStar said, telling me of the medical articles he saved, and the times they had sex in the middle of her cycle. She wanted to know more about Jim. She wanted me to tell her the story of who he really is, because he was a good person sometimes, and because he hurt people, and because she doesn't understand how the pieces of his frustrated personality fit together.

"He really wanted to be the ideal person, to have the perfect life, but he couldn't have it," SuperStar said as the café closes. They would sit together on the bed, SuperStar stoned, Hogue cold sober. He never smoked the weed he grew. He would lie in bed and lay out his plans for the future. Sometimes it felt good to lie next to him. "But more often he wasn't even looking at me," she remembered, with surprising bitterness. "He'd be staring off into the dreamworld that he created." Perhaps SuperStar was suspicious that Hogue's dreamworld didn't include her, or perhaps his descriptions of the future sounded like fantasies even to an eighteen-year-old girl. Their conversations left her feeling cold and alone. "He would keep talking and talking," she remembered sadly. "I don't think he was ever really there."

X. The Application

On my last evening in Telluride, I opened up a battered manila folder that I brought with me from New York, and began to read. The papers inside had been written two decades ago by an eighteen-year-old whose amazing life story had captivated nearly everyone who met him until it was finally revealed to be a lie. The folder and its contents had arrived at my office in New York through the offices of a lawyer who had finally obtained copies for me more than fifteen years after the originals were supposedly destroyed. Some of the documents were typewritten, and others were written by hand. There are about thirty pages in all. Together, they served as the blueprint for the greatest deception of Hogue's self-made career.

Once the papers arrived, and I identified them as genuine, I found other things to occupy my time. The essays and letters and lists inside seemed too important to read in a hurried way, before the stakes of Jim's case seemed clear, and before I felt sure about my own feelings about a subject whose defining feature was his opacity. Because Jim made himself so hard to read, and held so many parts of himself back, and became expert in inventing new identities, he made himself into a screen on which people could project their hopes and dreams. Jim could be anything that you wanted him to be. It was hard to say where my sympathy for Hogue came from, and that made me wary. Perhaps the idea of a continuous self was only a fiction that made it easier to enforce mortgage contracts and collect taxes. We become someone new every two or three years like a snake shedding its skin, and it is only a trick of the mind that supports the perception that we are the same person over any significant span of time. My belief that telling lies is destructive of the human community formed through language might be a freak of my own imagination and have little application to the life of a drifter who made himself up along the course of his own private and secretive journey.

I believed that my identification with James Hogue would help me understand him better. It would help me write a better story. It was a habit that Hogue had warned me against, and the fact that he was a liar and a thief didn't make his injunction any more or less binding. I would continue to see my life in his. I would continue to believe that the connection that I acknowledged was somehow valuable on a human level—a proof of my own laudable capacity for empathy. At the same time, I would also have to consider that any assumptions I made about Hogue might be reflections of my own selfish motives and preoccupations which had nothing whatsoever to do with my subject. Was Hogue afraid that I would see him for who he was? Was he annoyed by my invasion of his privacy? Did he court my attention because he wanted his story to be known? The answer to all of the above questions is "yes." For Hogue, the community of human beings that is formed through language was simply a figment of my imagination and the imaginations of other people like me. Week after week, the manila folder containing the plans for his greatest con lay unopened on my desk.

As the trial date approached, I headed off to Telluride with the folder stuffed in my green army duffle. I would read it when I felt ready. Once his sentence was handed down, and he refused for the last time to see me, I felt that it was time to look backwards through the wide lens of the telescope in the hopes that I might go back in time and see James Hogue whole, or glimpse the moment that led like all other moments to a place from which no escape is possible. I found more or less what I was looking for. I found myself rooting for him to succeed, even though I knew the story would turn out badly.

The folder contained a copy of an application to the Princeton University Class of 1992, complete with the required personal essays, lists of books, and proof of a 1410 SAT score. Other essential items, like a high school transcript and letters of recommendation from teachers, were missing.

Reading through the items in the folder, I was reminded again of how little connection the Ivy League selection process has to the ability or the inclination to endure the rigors of high-level academic work. Because we naturally abhor the geeky, antisocial personalities who tend to excel in the classroom and in the lab, America's most prestigious universities have turned the admissions process into a beauty contest rigged to favor the kinds of students that might look good on a television reality show—a wholesome racial and ethnic mix of pretty faces and talent-show winners. The often-celebrated search for lacrosse-playing cellists with 4.0 grade point averages and perfect SAT scores from disadvantaged neighborhoods also disguises a bushel of discriminatory policies that aim to cap the number of Jews and Asians and other minority groups who take education too seriously, in favor of the kinds of students that the admissions department and college alumni like better—namely, their own children.

Hogue's application to Princeton was both a carefully considered con and an inspired goof on the American college admissions process, an absurdist commentary on the larger absurdity of a system that would never have accepted him for who he was. Hogue gave the Princeton admissions office exactly what they wanted, reflecting their own self-serving mythology back to them in a mirror that he had crafted for that purpose. When they looked in the mirror, the face they would see was not his but their own—men and women of upstanding character and noble purpose. The fact that no similar student had ever applied to Princeton before might have cast some doubt on the true aim of the preferences they administered. Thanks to James Hogue, applying for admission to the Princeton Class of 1992 under the name Alexi Indris-Santana, the righteousness of their intentions could now be made plain.

"You will find that Part I of the Application for Admission is incomplete," Santana wrote. "I have not attended an organized school since my mother and I moved from Topanga, California to Europe in 1978," he explained. "I have been living independently here in the Mohave Desert since 1985, while my mother currently resides in Switzerland." Cleverly blending elite geography (Topanga, Switzerland), with his life in the Mohave Desert, Santana's story appealed to the admissions officers' yen for adventure while reassuring them that he came from a familiar, elevated cultural background that would help him fit in with his privileged classmates. By stressing the fact that he was living independently, apart from his mother, he also made himself eligible for increased levels of financial aid while removing the necessity to forge a set of documents from a second fictional character—his mother.

"Even though my formal education is lacking I do not consider myself disadvantaged for that reason," he wrote. Pronouncing himself to be "self-educated," he forswore any claim to inferior status, in language that might have been taken directly from Ben Franklin's diaries. Having sent clear signals that he should be given preference as a Hispanic student, he filled out the racial preference question on the application, "How would you describe yourself (check one)," with the coy notation, "I prefer not to respond." By checking the report of Hogue's SAT scores from the College Board (730 verbal, 680 math), Princeton could verify that the applicant was both "Mexican American" and a U.S. citizen.

The facts of his life were plain enough. Born on January 7,

1969, his father, Oscar Carlos Santana, was a self-employed pot-
ter; his mother, born Susan Vindriska, was a sculptress with an
undergraduate degree from the Universidad Nacional Autó-
noma de México and a graduate degree from the Pacific School
of Art. His permanent home address was the "state line" on the
Utah and Arizona border; he could be reached at post office box
1968 in St. George, Utah. He had worked as a mosaic-tile maker,
a cattle herder on the Lazy T ranch, a race-horse exerciser for a
man named Bud Payton, and as a construction worker. He was
interested in studying architecture, art, humanistic studies, visual arts, and science in human affairs, with a particular interest
in Western water policy as it related to farming and ranching.

But it was the details of Santana's life as a self-educated ranch
hand in the Mohave Desert that made the Princeton admissions
officers swoon. "As a person who spends several months tending
to a one-man herding station," Santana wrote, "I look forward to
excitement." He told Princeton about a "grueling, but wacky"
cross-country relay race called the "Levi's Ride and Tie," run by
teams consisting of a horse and two people. While one member
of the team sets off running, the other rides the horse ahead to a
predetermined spot where the runner finds it and then rides
ahead to the next hitching place, where his partner mounts the
horse. Santana had learned about the race from his friend Renee
Vera, who would drop by his herding station on her spirited Ara-
bian mare, Goodnuf.

What Santana offered Princeton was a storybook universe that
embodied all the requisite multicultural virtues at the same time
as it hearkened back to the mythic vistas of the unspoiled West.
There was something in his story for everyone in the Princeton
admissions office, from the most impassioned supporter of racial
diversity to the most dewy-eyed fan of Thomas Kinkade paintings and John Ford movies. "Each morning we raced the sun to
the top of the arduous trail out of Purgatory Canyon," Santana

wrote. The reward for winning was "to witness those spectacular few moments when the light first struck the Vermillion Cliffs. Even when the sun prevailed," he continued, "we were filled with the pride of getting to the top, then with the dread of descending the hazardously steep and rocky path."

If his metaphoric description of the glorious ascent to the summit and the dangers of the path below might be read by an enthusiastic literary critic as a nod to the thrills and dangers of the applicant's desire to better his class standing by applying to Princeton, the rest of the essay evoked his experience as a distance runner to explain what it was like to run a race. "Exhaustion creeps in slowly enough to dull a competitor's wits in a race this long," he wrote, "making it impossible to keep tabs on the other teams amid the constant relaying back and forth."

The occasional backstage cough and the suppressed laughter that runs throughout the essays are proof that the applicant, unlike so many others that year and since, was enjoying himself. Asked to "discuss more fully any academic or intellectual interest that is especially significant to you," he chose a book by a Nobel laureate physicist who taught at Princeton. *Surely You're Joking, Mr. Feynman!* made him want to learn more about physics, he wrote, noting that "Feynman loosely scatters references to science among the many anecdotes about safecracking, bongo playing and general fakery that he wants to be most known for." For an exceptionally suspicious mind, the choice of subject might have raised a wee bit of suspicion that Richard Feynman's disposition might be shared by the applicant himself. Having had his fun, the applicant attempted to squelch any such suspicions with a straight-faced description of how he had gone on to read Feynman's highly technical multivolume work *Lectures on Physics* in search of a deeper explanation of how the universe actually works.

"Soon I began to catch on that the trick is to sum up a complex situation in a few well-chosen words, just as his famous Feynman diagrams simplify subatomic encounters in a few squiggles and lines," the author explained. He playfully added, "I was able to approach the subject without worrying over every little detail precisely because someone as brilliant as Richard Feynman, B.S. MIT, PhD Princeton, distinguished professor of knowledge at Cal Tech could have 'stuff' as his favorite word."

What Feynman did in his writing about physics, Hogue would do by inventing the character of Alexi Indris-Santana, who could appeal to the prejudices of Ivy League admissions officers by translating the stops and starts of his own checkered academic career and his postcollegiate life as a drifter into a fairy tale that Princeton might understand: even the most advanced science was a way of approximating and communicating a reality that was actually quite different than what was being described. The most advanced minds, with the most advanced degrees from the most advanced colleges, believed that intellectual life was a sophisticated species of fraud. In conclusion, the applicant wrote, "The best that I can hope for from all of this is to emulate Feynman's attitude that science turns out to be essentially a long history of learning how not to fool ourselves." It was useful advice, which the Princeton admissions office had no intention of taking. In Alexi Indris-Santana, the self-educated ranch hand, they heard the siren song of the kind of experience that would surely be an asset to the Princeton Class of 1992.

To see a Princeton admission application as a contest of wits between faceless admissions officers and the cunning applicant is a common enough perception for seventeen- and eighteen-year-olds who are self-possessed enough to see the admissions process plain. Cloaked in officialese, the application is a contest between the young student and a living, breathing entity that seeks to sniff out cravenness and fear. The rules of the game are openly rigged in favor of wealthy graduates of elite schools and other favored categories of applicant who profess officially approved beliefs to signal to the college that they belong. Applicants clever or cynical enough to cast their lives in an acceptable mold will glide through with ease. Those who sweat too hard will find themselves at lesser colleges. Elite private schools advertise their success at the art of polishing and buffing the life stories of seventeen- and eighteen-year-old high school juniors and seniors to the proper gloss and sheen, either through the efforts of in-house staff or outside consultants who can be hired by wealthy parents at a price of however many thousands of dollars a month—a pittance compared to the difference that a Harvard or a Princeton diploma might make over the course of a lifetime. The job of recasting the life stories of wealthy teenagers is the kind of socially revealing occupation that Dickens or Balzac surely would have loved as a device in their fictions, as they would have also loved James Hogue, a young criminal with the brass to play against the Princeton admissions office and win.

"At this point in the application, we as admissions officers have gained some insight into the academic and extracurricular dimensions of your life," Princeton announced, in a gentle and faintly patronizing tone of assurance that would turn out to be entirely misleading. "But the description is still incomplete." In keeping with the tradition of the last fifty years, applicants were invited to reflect on an issue or experience that was significant to them, to be used as a Rorschach test by admissions officers eager to fill their quotas of hard-luck cases and perform whatever other acts of prestidigitation that the numbers game requires. Teenage applicants accustomed to cocktail-party culture and to the admissions process at the country clubs and other social institutions to which their parents belonged understand the purpose of open-ended invitations like the Personal Statement. The invitation to applicants to reveal themselves allows Princeton to choose the ones it actually wants and get rid of the others whose grades might be high enough and whose test scores might qualify them for admission but who "wouldn't fit in" at Princeton.

"This may be the most difficult part of the application," the application warned, before feeding applicants more of the doublespeak that more provincial or trusting applicants might be lured into taking to heart. "We do not ask a specific question or present a topic for this essay because the subject you choose tells us almost as much about you as the way you discuss it. We encourage you to choose your own topic and write about it in a way consistent with both the topic and your personality."

Hogue rose to the challenge with brio. "My advice to runaways, drop-outs, and gypsies in general can be found on the attached pages," he wrote. What followed was a personal statement that was as honest as anything that Hogue ever said or wrote, and that told the Princeton admissions office everything they needed to know about their applicant. "Would you like to be a wayfarer open to all experiences, unleashed from your possessions?" An opening mélange of beatnik clichés, which served to underline Hogue's purported youth and his lack of formal education, soon resolved itself into a heartfelt statement of purpose. "The person who strikes off is no hero, nor necessarily unconventional," he wrote, "but to a greater degree than most people, he or she thinks and acts independently. Yet along with that egofilled yea-saying," he continued, in a Whitmanesque vein, "you probably feel timid or unsure that it could be you: too straight, too late, too many responsibilities, whatever."

This was the voice of the James Hogue that his friends knew from late-night bull sessions in high school and from working construction in Las Vegas, a combination of con man and drifter, an adventurer who was in on the cosmic joke. A deadpan loner, a speaker of throwback hippie jive, a devotee of the open road.

"Obviously it does take something to kick around on the loose," he wrote.

This trip is for people who want to be free and adventurous, yet realize it won't come easily or without knocks. Your state of mind must allow for new experiences, for tolerance and humor, must be willing to accept some discomfort, insecurity and risk. Everybody, after all, makes their own scene. If you view the world as a hostile place, it will be, any friendly paranoiac can confirm that . . . you say yes to life, all of it, as opposed to the narrow sliver we get so content with.

Having set out his credo in language that Whitman and Kerouac would have appreciated, Hogue went on to describe the qualities that would allow a person to live the particular type of existence that he favored. Unlike so many seventeen- or eighteen-year-olds who might pledge allegiance to some similar creed, Hogue was willing to accept the privations that go along with the freedom to become someone new:

You'll lack luxuries, such as comfort and companionship, and at other times (or at the same time) you'll even miss out on necessities, such as food, sleep and shelter. You may be excited, bored, confused, desperate and amazed all in the same day. Or hour. It's not for comfort hounds or poolside fainthearts, whose thin convictions won't stand up to the problems that come along. The right state of mind allows you to take one thing at a time and deal with it. Approach this with the attitude, the knowledge and assurance that being poor and free is possible, valid and also rewarding.

You will find that going alone is a simple way. Right from the start, you don't have to depend on anyone for anything.

Loners are free men and women. Oneness is a very flexible state.

It is doubtful that anyone in the Princeton admissions office knew exactly what their prize recruit was talking about. But his outlook on life was certainly unique, and was no doubt different than that of most applicants for a place in the Class of 1992. "If you want to sleep in the snow or starve for a week, you just do it, and with a clear conscience," he explained. "I have been able to live in a manner that I wouldn't dream of imposing on anyone else. And there are times when this helps much."

The biggest problem with being a loner, Hogue wrote, was feeling lonely. While loneliness was admittedly difficult to tolerate, it also had its advantages, like making you more sensitive to your surroundings, and engraving experiences more deeply on your memory. But even the strongest person might wake up one morning and find that he had reached the limits of his endurance.

"If you have been lonely for as long as you can remember, the point of diminishing returns has probably been reached," he wrote. "You've learned enough about yourself. It was time to learn about other people. It was time to find a friend," he continued, "which, of course, is the other good thing about being lonely."

The absence of high school transcripts and the standard letters of recommendation troubled Princeton enough that a senior admissions officer named Katherine Popenoe wrote him a letter requesting more information in light of his "unusual circumstances." In lieu of grades and official references, Princeton asked for a statement describing Hogue's self-study, a list of books he had read, recommendations from two or three adults who had met Hogue before, and copies of papers or written exercises he had produced over the past two years.

"To the extent that you cannot supply documentation," Popenoe wrote, "you may be well advised to enroll in a local college and begin to acquire some formal educational credentials." While Princeton's emphasis on documentation made sense, the university was too eager to land a sub-four-minute miler with the made-for-Hollywood story to stick to its own requirements.

"Really, I don't have any papers to send unless you would like copies of essays that I wrote for other college applications," Hogue wrote. By mentioning other colleges, he was also threatening to take his precious life story—and his documented talents on the track—elsewhere. He sent along only a single recommendation, along with an eclectic reading list containing over a hundred books of the type that might naturally appeal to a child of the sixties and a self-educated ranch hand.

Typed on four single-spaced sheets of paper, the list was thoughtfully divided into idiosyncratic categories of the kind one might see pasted on the shelves in a rural bookstore. The mix of quality literature was impressive, with just enough howlers thrown in to qualify as the work of a self-educated adolescent. There was "Sociology, Political Science" (*All the President's Men* by Woodward and Bernstein; *Rules for Radicals* by Saul Alinsky; *Germinal* by Zola; *Die, Nigger, Die!* by H. Rap Brown; *The Truly Disadvantaged: The Inner City, The Underclass, and Public Policy* by the sociologist William Julius Wilson); "Women" (*Loose Change* by Sara Davidson; *The Left Hand of Darkness* by Ursula K. Le Guin, *The Mayflower Madam* by Sidney Biddle Barrows; *Voices from Women's Liberation*). There was "History" (*Bury My Heart at Wounded Knee* by Dee Brown, *Burr* by Gore Vidal; *The March of Folly*—spelled "Folley"—by Barbara Tuchman). Evidence that Hogue, like other applicants that year, had not read all the books on the list is provided by some notable eccentricities in categorization: *The Day of the Jackal* and *The Milagro Beanfield War* are both listed under "Travel," for example. In a touch that any survivor of high school English classes could appreciate, John Steinbeck received his own category, entitled "Steinbeck." The "Science and Technology" section included books by Richard Feynman, I. Bernard Cohen, Lewis Thomas, Stephen Jay Gould (*Ever Since Darwin; The Flamingo's Smile; The Mismeasure of Man*), John Gribbin (*In Search of Schrödinger's Cat*) and Douglas R. Hofstadter (*Metamagical Themas; Gödel, Escher, Bach; The Mind's I*). A section on "Survival Craft" (*Stalking the Wild Asparagus, Geology of the Great Basin, American Indian Utensils*) underlined Santana's background as a child of the West, as did his idiosyncratic choices in "Literature and Art" (*Wild Cow Tales* by Ben K. Green, *Cowboy and Western Songs* by Austin and Alta Fife). The list concluded with a rather cheekily titled list of "Good and Bad Books" that left readers guessing how the self-educated cowboy actually felt about a mixed bag of classics and contemporary titles including *In Watermelon Sugar* by Richard Brautigan, *Being There* by Jerzy Kosinski, *Oedipus Rex, King Lear, Red Storm Rising* by Tom Clancy, *The Sunset Bomber* by D. Kincaid, and *Adventures of Huckleberry Finn* by Mark Twain, who surely would have enjoyed Hogue's story.

The single supporting letter that arrived with the packet contained just enough information to suggest to a willing listener that Alexi Santana was exactly who he claimed to be. "Alexi worked for me as a livestock tender last summer. He was responsible for finding suitable pasture and water in an extremely sparse and rugged country," wrote George Cina, proprietor of the Lazy T Ranch at P.O. Box 681038 in Park City, Utah. "I was a little skeptical about hiring Alexi when I first met him because he is a very scrawny kid, even compared to other desert people. Others who know him assured me that he was harder than steel."

The letter may not have included any verifiable information or even a phone number at which George Cina could be reached, and no such information has ever been found by Princeton, me, or anyone else. But it proved to be enough to help seal the deal. "As for whether Alexi is smart enough to attend your school, I can't say," the author wrote. Alexi had worked on his ranch for a single summer, which was long enough for the fictional rancher to have formed a high opinion of his young employee's creativity, calmness, toughness, self-sufficiency, and his ability to withstand bad weather and work hard. "Alexi is a very quiet person and I never could tell if he was book-smart," he wrote:

> To be able to spend weeks alone with a herd takes somebody who is either too stupid to be bothered or a person who has a head full enough of ideas not to get bored. Usually, the stupid person fails miserably at some point. I have the feeling that Alexi is probably one of those geniuses, at least he is unusual.

It was his aim to help Alexi in any way possible, the author added, "just as if he were one of my own kids. I recommend him without qualification, because he deserves it."

Princeton

I. The Locker

On March 30, 1988, a police detective named Matt Jacobson arrived at the Secure Storage facility in St. George, Utah, with a warrant to search for high-end racing bicycles, tools, and other parts that had been stolen from a man in California several months before. Raising the corrugated steel door of locker No. 100, the detective flicked a switch to illuminate a sixty-square-foot area with aluminum walls, no windows, and a bare concrete floor. On the floor of the locker he saw the stolen bicycle frames and parts, a Rolex submariner watch, papers, letters, a sleeping bag, and other personal effects. The detective guessed correctly that the thief had been living in the shed, perhaps for months.

Standing next to Jacobson in the locker, the bicycle maker Dave Tesch blew on his hands and stepped forward to identify the bicycles and tools as his own. The glare of the artificial light bouncing off the aluminum walls lent a claustrophobic intensity to the windowless space. The temperature in the locker was well below freezing, and Tesch had been up all night after driving seven hours from San Marcos, California, up to St. George. As he later explained, "I was pretty darn mad and also somewhat obsessed."

A stocky, olive-skinned man with a hangdog look, soft brown eyes, and self-inflicted tattoos covering his forearms, Tesch was a true obsessive who cared about very little else in the world aside from building bicycles. Starting with an initial investment of $15,000, the proceeds from the sale of some Chagall plates he picked up while serving in the Navy in Florida, he had built the Tesch Bicycle Company in San Marcos into one of the elite small manufacturers in the world. The company produced approxi-

mately five hundred bicycles per year for the growing community of cyclists who preferred American-made bikes to the undeniably light, fast, and beautiful machines made by the famous
European racing houses like Bottecchia, Frejus, and Colnago.
Purists complained that Tesch's bicycles were too heavy, and
that they never quite achieved the same marriage of function,
form, and flat-out speed as the Italians. Yet it is also true that the
Tesch Bicycle Company, working out of its tiny, handmade space
in the wilds of Southern California, was one of only a handful of
American companies capable of meeting the Europeans on
equal ground. While the Europeans built their bikes for varied
and rugged courses that meandered over country lanes, up and
down mountains, and through cobblestone streets, Tesch built
bikes for the American racing circuit, where the races were
shorter and faster and the turns were sharper. Adapting the
magic formulas of the European makers for the American racing
market, Tesch took the wheelbase of the Raleigh riders and used
a fork (the front part of the frame, which holds the front wheel)
with thirty-five millimeters of rake (the distance between the
wheel axle and the extension of the steering axis), an adjustment
that made the bikes easier to handle, and allowed taller American riders to cut corners just like their shorter European competitors.

In the 1980s, the small number of American craftsmen capable
of making world-class racing bikes clustered together in one of
two places. Some lived in or around Chester, Connecticut, which
was home to Albert Eisentrecht, the European émigré designer
who did more than any other man to bring the industrial art of
making high-end racing bicycles to America. On the West Coast,
the town of San Marcos, California, was home to Tesch, Dave
Moulton of Masi, and Moulton's former co-worker Brian Bayliss.
Encouraged by the surprise gold-medal victory of the American

cyclist Alexi Grewal at the 1984 Olympics in Los Angeles, the Californians expanded their trade in custom bikes throughout the following decade. A company known as Merlin made racing bikes with bare titanium frames. In Glendale, California, a company called Santana made tandem bikes, rescuing the bicycle built for two from the archives of American pop culture and winning 80 percent of that specialized market.

Charging $3,000 and up for a custom-designed model, Tesch liked to compare his bikes to Ferraris; one of his most popular colors was a Ferrari red that he copied directly from a showroom paint sample. While Tesch never got rich from the uncertain business of selling custom-made bicycles, he thrived on the knowledge that he was working at the top of his specialized craft. He loved driving up to the Tesch Bicycle Company with his Doberman pinscher in the back seat of his old Volvo, getting out of the car, hearing the click of the key as it turned in the lock, letting the dog loose, and turning up the radio. He loved going to work every morning believing that he made the best racing bikes in the world.

So when Tesch opened the door of his shop one morning in October 1987 to find that someone had kicked over a turbine vent, jumped down through a hole in the roof, landed on top of the paint table, and made off with more than $20,000 worth of custom frames, parts, and tools, his anger at the theft was compounded by the knowledge that he could ill afford the loss. A similar break-in had been reported at the custom shop owned by Brian Bayliss a few months before. Since rumor had it that the break-in was an inside job, Tesch leapt with characteristic but misplaced certainty to the conclusion that Bayliss had burglarized his shop. Tesch's judgment was less sure than usual. He was suffering the effects of a bad fall on a bike that had sent him into a coma for three days and deprived him of his sense of smell. He was also taking Halcion, a psychoactive drug that has been reported to have striking and bizarre effects on the moods of its users.

In fact, the thief was someone Tesch knew well. For the previous few summers, Tesch had worked as an instructor at Jim Davis's Vail Cross Training camp, which offered amateur and professional athletes the chance to enjoy a week in Vail, Colorado, under the tutelage of famous track-and-field stars like Scott "the Terminator" Molina and the pioneering American distance runner Frank Shorter, who won gold at the 1976 Olympics in Montreal. The instructors also included James Hogue, a sub-four-minute miler who, according to the camp's promotional literature, had earned a PhD in bioengineering from Stanford University, where he worked as a professor during the academic year.

Hogue stood out from his fellow instructors in other ways as well. His body fat percentage was said to be only 6 percent, a remarkably low number even for a world-class athlete, and his shy, diffident manner and youthful face made him appear more like a college student than a professor. His youthful appearance was increased by his regular uniform of a windbreaker or a warm-up jacket with a T-shirt or running singlet underneath and a pair of Nike or New Balance running shoes on his feet, as if to suggest that at any moment he might run a ten- or fifteen-mile race. His training methods were often unorthodox. He drank a mixture of mustard and Perrier during races, and he lit up a cigarette after crossing the finish line, as the other runners looked on in horror.

Frank Shorter was suspicious of Hogue, and he voiced his suspicions to his fellow instructors. But somehow the Olympic gold medalist's opinions never took hold. Hogue had a way of endearing himself to his students, many of whom were doctors, lawyers, and corporate executives in their everyday lives, and who welcomed a chance to learn new training methods from a top runner who was also a professor at Stanford. Hogue soon earned a reputation for modesty and kindness to go with his prestigious academic position. When asked direct questions, he looked down at the ground, and then responded in the fewest possible number of words. When a woman at the camp wanted to buy a bicycle that she couldn't really afford, Hogue got her the frame for a nominal price. The other instructors never guessed that Hogue was not a professor at Stanford, or that he had awarded his PhD in bioengineering to himself. Nor did anyone suspect that Hogue might be responsible for a rash of thefts that plagued the camp that summer. (The expensive bicycle frame that Hogue sold to the student on the cheap turned out to have been stolen several months earlier from a bike shop run by the father of Alexi Grewal, the 1984 Olympic gold medalist.)

Dave Tesch's live-in girlfriend, Meg Barry, was also suspicious of Hogue. A gifted gem cutter, she spent her professional life examining precious stones through a jeweler's loop and under a microscope, minutely evaluating their color and size while searching out flaws that might adversely affect their value. She was not at all happy when Hogue showed up in San Marcos one afternoon and knocked on the door of the house she shared with Tesch. Parking his truck outside the house, which he occasionally used to take showers, Hogue came and went, helping out around the shop, sleeping in his truck, and otherwise leading a life that appeared to have little in common with that of a normal Stanford professor. When someone attempted to break into the house, Barry immediately thought of Hogue.

The mystery of the theft that nearly destroyed Tesch's business remained unsolved until March 1988, when a young wannabe surfer from Utah named Bruce Stucki stopped by on his way back home with a story that he thought might interest the bike builder. Stucki and his friends were Mormons who loved to race bicycles. He told Tesch that one of his friends had recently been at a party in St. George, Utah, where an acquaintance had whipped out a Mitsutoyo metric dial caliper, a specialized tool, engraved with Tesch's name, which Stucki had immediately recognized. When Stucki returned to Utah, he informed Detective Matt Jacobson of his discovery. Jacobson called Tesch, who provided him with physical descriptions and serial numbers for the frames that had been stolen from his shop.

Jacobson, who was not especially interested in bike racing, was particularly disturbed by a collection of athletic trophies he found in the locker, which had been awarded to Hogue for races he had won while running under an assumed name. "They were obviously meant for an eighteen-year-old," the detective remembered, when I visited with him in Utah. For Jacobson, who now specializes in investigating crimes against children, the thief had committed a particularly disturbing sin. He had entered a race under a false name and deprived younger runners of the places they had rightfully won. Within minutes of Jacobson's arrival, Hogue walked up to the storage locker. Jacobson placed him in handcuffs and read him his rights. "I remember telling him how appalled I was that someone would do this," the detective recalled. "And it didn't seem to shake him or even faze him at all."

The only hints as to James Hogue's state of mind on the day of his arrest survive in the form of two photographs taken upon his arrival at the police station. The photographs show a frightened-looking young man between twenty-five or thirty years of age staring into the camera. He looks like someone who has spent weeks or months living in the woods or on the floor of a bus station. A growth of beard obscures the shape of his face and his thin, boyish features. Sleeplessness, pain, and nervous exhaustion have settled in the hollows beneath his eyes.

As it turned out, Hogue's theft from the Tesch Bicycle Company was the key to a far more intricate deception, the clues to which were neatly laid out in the storage locker in St. George. The correspondence there showed that Hogue had been occupied with a larger, more imaginative goal than disposing of the stolen bikes. He had been dreaming of a better life, to be led by a person who was not James Hogue. The product of careful research and planning, this new identity would be backed up by newspaper clippings and trophies that bore the name Alexi Santana—a self-educated Nevada cowboy who could run a mile in just under four minutes and, according to the correspondence found in the shed, had applied for admission to some of America's finest universities, including Yale, Harvard, Stanford, Princeton, and Brown.

"It was a weird, unbelievable story," Tesch recalled. "Like 'I was born a poor black child,' the old Steve Martin routine." The name Alexi Santana also rang a bell: it sounded like a combination of the first name of Alexi Grewal, the Olympic cycling gold medalist, and the surname Santana, the tandem-bike manufacturer. In the weeks leading up to his trial, Hogue called Tesch from jail, hoping to convince him to drop the charges. Tesch refused to return the calls. Instead he called a woman who lived in Provo, Utah, whose name he no longer remembers, but who might have been Hogue's sister, or his girlfriend, who had custody of Hogue's blue Toyota pickup truck. As his business sunk deeper in debt, Tesch took to calling this woman again and again, leaving angry messages on her answering machine. She called back one night when Tesch was already in bed, after taking his nightly dose of Halcion. Half asleep, and in the grip of a powerful and disorienting drug, Tesch picked up the phone and began ranting and raving, pouring out a year's worth of rage at having been fooled by his friend and demanding title to Hogue's truck. The woman refused.

Detective Jacobson called Stanford University to inform the university that the applicant Alexi Santana was actually a twenty-eight-year-old drifter named James Hogue, who had been impersonating a Stanford professor and was now on his way to jail in Utah. Hogue pleaded guilty to the theft and was given a sentence of one to five years in prison. A story appeared in the April 17, 1988, edition of the *San Jose Mercury News* duly noting that police had also "found evidence that Hogue, using the name 'Alexi Santana,' was corresponding with Ivy League universities about athletic scholarships." Years later, Detective Jacobson simply did not remember whether or not he had called the other universities with which Santana had been corresponding to warn them that the applicant was an impostor.

II. The Lottery

Alexi Santana's memorable application to Princeton University was one of nearly fourteen thousand for twelve hundred places in the Class of 1992. Once, when Fred Hargadon, the head of the Princeton admissions office, was asked to describe the perfect candidate for admission, he answered with the name of a fictional character, Huck Finn. Most students selected for admission probably have less in common with the illiterate son of a violent alcoholic than with his diplomatic young friend Tom Sawyer. Still, Hargadon's answer does neatly summarize the virtues that Princeton looks for in at least some of its applicants—originality, self-reliance, and the kind of "diverse life experiences" that might keep the school's Tom Sawyers entertained.

Santana's score of 1410 on the SAT was well above the average of students admitted to Princeton, and his Hispanic-sounding surname likely recommended him for special consideration as a minority applicant. But his personal essay, the story of a self-educated ranch hand who read Plato under the stars, lifted his application to the top of the pile. Santana had "trained on his own in the Mohave Desert, where he herds cattle for a living (mostly in a canyon called 'Little Purgatory')," the admissions office reported, in a private letter sent to wealthy alumni in the early summer, after the Class of 1992 had been accepted. "On a visit to campus in March, he slept indoors for the first time in ten years."

As his application was being read by members of the Princeton admissions office, Hogue was living in the storage locker and in his sister Theresa's house in St. George, and spending long afternoons in the public library, researching the published statistics that tell who is admitted to universities like Princeton and why.

The great majority of every Princeton class, Hogue discovered, was made up of the children of parents whom most Americans would describe as "rich." About a fifth of every Princeton class consisted of students whose fathers or mothers went to Princeton; the SAT scores of these "legacies" were often well below average for their class. Applicants from sparsely populated states like Nevada, Montana, and Wyoming received preference over students from competitive high schools in cities like New York, a system dated to the end of the First World War, a time when officials at Harvard, Princeton, and Yale were working hard to find an answer to what they called the "Jewish question." They arrived at a formula for "geographical distribution" (now styled "geographical diversity") that would increase the number of "white" students on their campuses while radically decreasing the numbers of Jews.

By accepting the barefoot shepherd from the Nevada desert, the university hoped to demonstrate that a Princeton degree was proof of some inherent personal merit, rather than a cunning device by which members of the American professional elite might pass on their social status and earning power to their children. Yet even a cursory look at the numbers revealed that Princeton's sense of itself as a pillar of meritocracy was no less a fiction than the story of the self-educated ranch hand who taught himself to read Plato under the stars. The America of the nineties was a nation in which elite educational credentials were more tightly correlated with social and economic status than ever before; a Princeton degree was a passport to jobs at name investment banks, venture-capital firms, management consultancies, and high-tech companies. Most students accepted to Princeton were the children of parents who had graduated from Princeton or some similarly exclusive college, who worked professional-class jobs, lived in expensive houses in exclusive neighborhoods, and earned incomes of $100,000 a year or more, placing them within the top 10 percent, and often the top 1 percent, of money earners in America. These lessons were hardly lost on the lonely drifter, whose ability as a runner was matched by his talent for telling stories that might take him where he wanted to go.

III. The Loneliness of the Long-Distance Runner

The story of the young Huck Finn from Nevada with high SAT scores and a Hispanic surname had a particular appeal for Princeton's track coach, Larry Ellis, who had coached the 1984 American Olympic men's track team and was the first black man to assume a head coaching job at an Ivy League university. Ellis was already impressed by the press clippings and race results that Santana had sent in along with his application, which showed the eighteen-year-old ranch hand beating his competition on a cinder track with times as fast as or faster than those run by Princeton's older, more experienced athletes. In fact, when Ellis first heard the story of the young man who had taught himself to run in the desert, he was so impressed that he shared it with his wife. "Larry was so surprised about an athlete who was able to roam throughout the country, practically educating himself," his widow, Shirley Ellis, recalled. "The boy's mother supposedly was in Europe; she was an artist. His father had died. He lived on an Indian reservation and was a very active person."

Ellis did not care that Santana's background might strike many people at Princeton as unusual. He urged Santana to visit Princeton, and sent him a round-trip ticket. When the assistant track coach, Fred Samara, heard that the runner was coming to visit, he took a member of the team, Jon Luff, aside. "Santana's coming out here," Luff remembered him saying, "and I want you to run as hard as you possibly can, every day, the entire time he's here. And I want you to come back Monday and report to me, and tell me exactly what you think."

Luff, a dark, remarkably handsome young engineer who could work as a Ralph Lauren model if engineering ever gets boring, came to Princeton from Colorado; as a fellow Westerner, the coaches reasoned, he would be able to relate to Santana and show him around campus. When Santana arrived in early March, he went to the field house to meet with the coaches. Luff met him outside.

"He always wore a hat, probably to hide the fact that he was going bald," Luff observed later. The applicant was short and small and only weighed a hundred and twenty pounds, and it was easy to believe that he was eighteen or nineteen years old. He had a slight build and a soft handshake, and he kept his eyes firmly focused on the ground. Dressed in a simple and unvarying uniform of jeans, a white T-shirt, a windbreaker, and cowboy boots or running shoes, depending on the time of day, he made a good first impression on Luff.

Over the weekend that followed, any doubts that might have existed about the young runner's talent were put to rest. One of the better runners on the Princeton team, Luff tried his best to beat Santana. "He could have run thirty minutes for ten thousand meters. He probably could have run fourteen minutes for five thousand, if he wanted to," Luff said. "I couldn't crop him. I couldn't really even tire him out. And so, of course, I came back and said, 'The guy's for real. He can really run.' "

To understand who the applicant was, and how he was able to succeed, for a time, in such an audacious imposture, it is necessary to step back for a moment from our story and think about the one true constant in Hogue's scattered life, which was not his true name or even his talents for imposture but the habit of running long distances at a pace that only a few human beings on the planet could match. Distance running offers almost no material rewards and demands a dedication so complete that it is hard for many world-class runners to hold down regular jobs. It is normal for distance runners to cry, scream, vomit, and even urinate

on themselves during races. Push beyond those barriers often
enough and knees swell and tendons snap, leading to chronic injuries that can make it hard for distance runners to walk, let alone
run. What running offers in exchange is the euphoric pleasure of
the runner's high. Anyone who has engaged in even mildly intense physical activity, like jogging, playing tennis, or working out
at the gym, has experienced some version of this state, in which
the brain is flooded by mood-elevating chemicals that wash away
the daily residues of anxiety, boredom, and fear. For runners, the
dream-like state induced by running ten or fifteen miles can become necessary to their sense of well-being, and as potent an ad-
diction as any drug.

"One of the things I used to like to do," Jon Luff remembered,
"was run in the dark. And you can go out and run really hard in
the dark and you actually don't feel like you have a body. You feel
like you're just this head moving around, because you are in such
good shape that you don't even really feel the road, and you can
just get into a rhythm where you're sort of ethereal in this weird
way. You're just kind of out there, floating around. It's a bizarre
feeling."

Other aspects of the runner's high can best be compared to the
effects of daily meditation, or any other discipline that demands
that the practitioner subordinate all other parts of their life to a
thirst for the transcendence that only their chosen discipline can
provide. For Luff, the highs that distance running offered were
matched by the promise of self-sufficiency, of an activity that created its own sense of meaning and absolute necessity:
"To be completely absorbed on a daily basis, and to be completely happy doing something that by definition needs or requires nothing."

The world of long-distance runners is filled with people who
dedicate their lives to the experience that Luff describes, spend-

ing two months here and three months there, moving from one runner's town to the next, spending summers in Boulder, Colorado, and winters in Southern California, without steady work or sustaining relationships, willing to sacrifice almost anything for a taste of the distilled transcendence that is available to those who are willing to train their bodies and minds by running hard for ten to fifteen miles a day. Familiar aspects of everyday reality and behavior are stripped bare. The runner's mind, operating in a void for many hours every day, becomes more and more practiced in distilling things down to their essence, and to enduring great extremities of pain.

The two runners ran together all that first weekend, and would later become close friends. Santana was very different from the person Luff had expected to meet. He was gentle and inquisitive. As he discovered things about Luff, he offered new stories that expanded the territory they had in common, like their shared love for the mountains. He looked forward to seeing his new friend in September.

Luff brought Santana to his interview with Katherine Popenoe at West College, the ancient red brick building where the Princeton admissions office is housed. The two met there for approximately an hour, and then Popenoe accompanied the applicant downstairs.

"You know what?" Luff offered to the neatly dressed, middleage woman who held Santana's fate in her hands. "He's really a unique person."

"Well, yeah," Popenoe answered. "He's very well read." Santana's application suggested that he knew Norwegian; Popenoe had lived in Norway and spoke Norwegian, and the two had exchanged a few words in that language. The admissions officer also quizzed him about the long list of books he had submitted with his application, with satisfactory results.

Luff found himself envying his new friend. "This is a really strange process," he joked to Popenoe. "This is great. If I knew about this, I would have skipped high school."

As he turned to leave, another question occurred to him. "What kind of people do this?" he asked.

Popenoe's answer was matter-of-fact. "Well," she said, "I really only get this type of application from ex-cons or people in prison."

Several weeks later, Alexi Santana received, via a post office box in St. George, a letter informing him that his application to Princeton had been accepted. His total family contribution would be $2,010 ($1,340 from his summer savings, $170 from the sale of his artworks, $500 from his parents). Princeton would give him a grant of $12,730. His tuition, fees, and other expenses amounted to $21,100—a sum that exceeded the take-home pay that the average American adult would make that year. The difference would come from federal loans, a Pell Grant, and an on-campus job.

While Princeton's offer of financial aid was undeniably generous, the timing of their acceptance letter could not have been less convenient. On March 30, 1988, two weeks before the letter from Princeton arrived in his post office box, James Hogue appeared in court in St. George and pled guilty to receiving bicycle frames and tools that had been stolen from Tesch's shop in San Marcos. On May 19, when 1,134 other members of the Princeton Class of 1992 were glorying in their acceptance to one of America's most prestigious universities and looking forward to their last summer before college, Hogue was sentenced to a maximum term of five years in prison; he would serve twelve months.

On the brink of a breathtaking escape from his life as a drifter and a petty thief living in a storage locker by the side of a highway in Utah, Hogue had been ambushed by the past. He marked his first week in the Utah State Prison in Draper by writing a letter to Katherine Popenoe at the Princeton admissions office. "Dear Ms. Popenoe," he wrote on the thin white-lined paper provided to inmates by the State of Utah Corrections Department. "Your offer caused a great deal of excitement and anticipation in my little world. If you could only know what ideas filled my mind. . . ."

The author's chief motive and preoccupation was his desire to keep Alexi Santana's admission to Princeton alive while his creator was in jail. He would be forced to defer Princeton's offer for one year, he wrote. A close friend of his had run into legal problems, and he had spent all his money in order to help him. Now, his mother in Switzerland was suffering from a serious blood ailment, and he needed to comfort her in any way that he could. "I'm just sick to think that my withdrawl [sic] has deprived another candidate of a place in the class," he wrote, in what perhaps might be taken as an admission of the effect that his deception might have had on another deserving candidate.

At the same time, being locked up in jail was a powerful reminder there were worse things in life than gaining admission to Princeton by making up a new name for yourself and a silly story about a self-educated shepherd who ran barefoot through the desert canyons. "I have come to see how precious and coveted these spots are," he wrote. "I don't think I appreciated this enough before now." Here, at least, there is no reason not to take Hogue at his word. His visit to Princeton a few months earlier must have seemed like a memory of paradise compared to the realities of being locked up in a cell in Utah. While he would not be in touch directly for a while, he warned, Princeton could reach him through his girlfriend, who would forward any correspondence. The address he gave was a post office box in Park City, Utah, that belonged to his sister Theresa, who had hosted Hogue off and on after he fled from California, and claimed to be ignorant of his deceptions. By the end of his letter, Hogue was feeling good enough about his chances to indulge himself in some sly Latin wordplay.

"*Ad astra per aspera,*" the self-educated cowboy from Nevada signed off—"to the stars through difficulties."

It is possible that some prep-school Latin scholar in the Princeton admissions department was able to translate the motto, and relate it to the difficulties that Santana outlined in his letter. But it would have taken a true license plate addict to notice that the Latin phrase that appeared above Santana's signature was the official motto of the state of Kansas, which is nearly flat and very far away from the mountains where Santana claimed to have herded sheep.

No one in the Princeton admissions office got the joke. No one ever saw the article in the *San Jose Mercury News* mentioning that a thief had been applying to Ivy League colleges under the pseudonym of Alexi Indris-Santana. The phone calls that track coach Larry Ellis received that spring had not come from Santana. They had come from James Hogue, a twenty-nine-year-old inmate in the Utah state prison system whose natural ability as a runner was matched by a talent for telling stories that might take him where he wanted to go.

IV. A Bicycle Built for Two

Alexi Indris-Santana arrived at Princeton in August of 1989, six weeks before classes began, to work out on the track and to attend an early orientation program. There he was interviewed by Harvey Yavener, a reporter for the Trenton *Times*. Coach Ellis had told Yavener about the barefoot runner from a ranch in Nevada, and he thought that it would make an excellent feature for his paper. The interview took place early in August, a month when reporters on the college-sports beat are always grateful for a good story.

Dressed in running sneakers, jeans, and a white oxford shirt, the young Princeton freshman seemed confident but shy. His eyes were hidden by a pair of dark sunglasses. He had the weather-beaten features of a person who had led a hard life, who had slept outdoors and worked as a cowboy. "You have to sit under a black Arizona sky at night to know what the Milky Way really is," Hogue told Yavener. "There are times I yearn for those open spaces. But running the backwoods here, I've found how beautiful this Princeton area can be," he continued, in a soft, wistful voice, across the conference room table in the track-team office.

Hogue had lived in Switzerland, Costa Rica, Jamaica, Morocco, and several Western states, he said. He had been educated at home. "It's not that unusual," he told Yavener, before providing the most complete recorded version of Alexi Santana's mythical life. "At least, not when I was young in California. I went to nursery school and kindergarten, and then my parents decided they'd teach me at home. You have to set up a private school. I learned to read early and always had a lot of books. Some days, I'd read from morning to night. I learned some French and Italian. I never have had a TV, but I listened to a lot of music. I'd go to librarians, and they'd help me find the books I needed."

Yavener had been covering college sports in southern New Jersey for nearly forty years. He had never heard a story like this one before. The Princeton freshman had started running only two years earlier, while working as a wrangler on a thousand-square-mile ranch in Arizona, where he spent weeks with just his books, his horse, the cows, and a radio for company. "I just started to run around the canyons in a pair of old tennis shoes, nothing fanatical," he explained. "I think I might have the talent to become a winning runner in college. But those stories about my coming in with impressive times, they're just hearsay."

Barely three months had elapsed since James Hogue had been released from prison in Utah. After having violated his parole by leaving the state, he was now Alexi Santana, a self-educated ranch hand, a gifted runner, and easily the most interesting member of the Princeton Class of 1993.

"I'm looking forward to this adventure," he told the readers of the Trenton *Times*. "I expect to spend a lot of happy hours here in the library, but happy hours in other things, too."

Santana's father was dead and his mother was ill, he said. He had no fixed address. But, as he told the reporter that afternoon in August, he had finally found a home. "If anyone asks," he said, "I'll tell them I'm from Princeton."

V. The Roommates

Like most incoming freshmen, Ben Richardson arrived on campus that September with new clothes, a computer, a selection of favorite books and records, and the phone numbers of high school friends who would be attending other colleges. He also brought with him the packet of material that Princeton had sent with his acceptance letter, including the little card that gave the names and addresses of his new roommates. Over the summer, Richardson had talked by phone with Avshalom Yotam of Palo Alto, California, and Austin Nahm of New York. His third roommate, Alexi Santana, did not have a phone number or address listed on the card.

Richardson's new rooms were on the ground floor of Holder Hall, a Gothic stone pile constructed around a pleasant grassy courtyard during the decade following World War I. Arriving on campus more than a week before most of his class, Richardson saw a light in one of the windows of his suite. The next morning, as he moved his stuff into the room, he met Alexi Santana, who was just returning from his morning run. Santana told him that he ran ten miles a day. He had worked on a ranch. His father had been killed in a car crash, and his mother had recently died of leukemia.

Over the next few days, and the year that followed, it was hard not to look for clues that might further illuminate his roommate's unusual story. Santana's room was neat and filled with books and CDs, and the Mexican wool blanket on his bed was always tucked in flat. At an age when few students in college are inclined or accustomed to making their beds, his roommate's practice struck Richardson as strange.

"I remember asking, 'Alexi, your bed's always made up very neatly, do you get up and make it every day or what?' " Richardson said.

"No," Santana answered. "I sleep on the floor."

Next to Santana's bed was a picture of a skier kicking out his legs and raising a curtain of powdered white snow in front of the camera. Richardson was curious about the picture, too.

"So who's the photo of," he asked.

"Oh, it's me," Santana answered.

"How did you get someone to take a photo like that?" Richardson wondered.

"Oh, I was doing some stuff, doing some stunts."

"What were you doing stunts for?

"A movie."

Richardson also knew that his roommate was an exceptionally gifted student who had cracked the curve on an exam for a required class in chemistry that notoriously gave freshmen fits. According to the results posted for that exam, Santana's score was fully two standard deviations above the mean. "Those tests are written for babies," Santana told him. "Princeton babies their students. It's incredibly easy."

Such attention-seeking comments were rare. Santana avoided direct eye contact when he spoke. His room was bare of pictures of friends or family. He didn't have a photograph of his mother who had died of leukemia in Switzerland the previous year, and no one from outside the university ever called him or wrote. Still, he rarely seemed lonely. He turned the closet in his room into a wine cellar and hosted wine and cheese parties for groups of eight or ten freshmen women, whom he regaled with stories of his adventures living and working in exotic places. His roommates were not invited to his parties. With his mature demeanor and sophisticated tastes, he soon earned the nickname Sexy Alexi.

The stories that Richardson heard from his classmates were even wilder. Santana had skied in the Olympics. He had dropped from a helicopter and turned double back flips in a Peter Markle ski comedy called *Hot Dog*. He had built a powerful computer from scratch. As Princeton freshmen engaged in a class-wide game of telephone, the stories returned to Richardson with even more outlandish details, some of which even turned out to be true. A freshman named Jill Williford and her friends rented *Hot Dog* one evening and watched the movie through until the end, where they saw their famous classmate's name in the credits.

There is something undeniably thrilling about the myth of Alexi Santana, and about the cocksure arrogance with which a drifter was able to make up a new life for himself from scratch and get As at Princeton. It also helps to remember that in reality he was a twenty-eight-year-old man who was competing with students who were ten years younger than he was. While Santana's creator had never enjoyed the privilege that many of his classmates had enjoyed throughout their young lives, he was highly intelligent and had attended college before. He had come to Princeton, he told anyone who would listen, in order to find a wife.

Santana was not particularly friendly with Ben Richardson, and he seems to have actively avoided any opportunities for conversation with his other roommate, Avshalom Yotam. Years later, Yotam would remember only that the person he shared a suite with for a year was an orphan, that he kept the door to his room closed, and that he often wore odd-looking or ragged clothes.

"I picture him as sort of small-framed, a little bit hunched over," he later remembered. "He was in very good physical shape. But he always walked hunched over, with his long hair sort of hiding his face. So you never really saw his face, even when he was right there in front of you."

Communication between the two roommates was so slight that Yotam would later remember that during the course of two semesters they had had only one conversation that lasted longer than thirty seconds.

"I remember pretty distinctly lying on the couch in the common room, and at some point, either he asked me or it somehow came up, and I told him that I was from Palo Alto," he said.

"You know, Palo Alto is a really nice place," Santana remarked.

"Oh, have you been there?"

"Yes, I've been there," he answered. "It's a really nice place."

Yotam tried to get his roommate to expand on his impressions of his hometown and whatever time he might have spent there, but Santana didn't want to talk. He was a private person, he said. They never spoke about Palo Alto again. As far as Yotam can remember, his roommate never spoke to him again on any subject for the rest of the year.

Under most ordinary circumstances, the desire for privacy is unattainable for most Princeton freshmen, who sleep two to a room in aging accommodations that have little in common with the glossy pictures in the admissions brochures. Santana would realize his desire thanks to a tragic accident involving a fourth roommate, Austin Nahm. The day after he arrived at Princeton, Nahm had left campus on a freshman outdoor orientation trip, was hit by a speeding truck, and died. When Santana heard that his roommate was dead, he broke down and cried for perhaps ten minutes.

Reporters soon arrived at room 141, and the university sent counselors to help the three remaining roommates cope with the shock. But although Santana's emotions ran deep, he showed no inclination to talk to reporters or to share his feelings in any therapeutically approved way. Perhaps he was moved by the senseless death of someone so young, or perhaps he was feeling the stress of maintaining his invented self. Perhaps he felt some guilt that his roommate was dead while he himself lived on in borrowed clothing. Or perhaps his uncharacteristically emotional response had something to do with another consequence of the accident: for the rest of the year, as he went to classes and made new friends, alive to the possibility that at any moment the mask could slip and reveal his true face, Alexi Santana would have a single room at Princeton all to himself.

VI. The Legend of Alexi Santana

Looking back years later, members of the Princeton Class of 1993 understood the story of Alexi Santana as a puzzling crime, as an abuse of the admissions process, or as a weird occurrence that had little to do with their own lives. Some expressed compassion for their former classmate. All remembered that they had been fooled. They told his story to strangers on airplanes, to girls they asked out to dinner, and to friends from Princeton who knew the story, too. The story of Alexi Santana would continue to shadow their lives long after they left Princeton. It was something that the Class of '93 shared in common. All remembered that they had been fooled.

When I first corresponded with Christine Zandliviet by e-mail she was working for the Office of the High Representative in Bosnia-Herzegovina. She had arrived at Princeton early her freshman year for a foreign-student orientation program when she met Santana, who told her about his mother, who was living in Switzerland. "He mentioned something about Interlaken, and something about Basel," she remembered. "But he was never specific, like he didn't want to be pinned down into saying where his mother was physically, in which sanitorium, or where he had traveled in Switzerland. I myself had been living in Geneva, and had traveled around, and so I wanted to share some experiences."

It was strange that Santana didn't seem to know elementary words in German or French. Still, his manner was always calm and relaxed, in a way that made it easy to picture him as the child of hippie parents.

"In a way he was quite a loner. But in a way he was also very so-

ciable. He was a very flexible person. He could fade into a group
and not stand out."

•

Elizabeth Eaton is an attorney with Wilentz, Goldman & Spitzer,
a law firm in northern New Jersey. "I remember one evening when we were watching the news
with a bunch of other people in the Rocky common room," she
says, using familiar shorthand for Rockefeller, one of the university's seven residential colleges. "And he mentioned that he
didn't have a television set where he grew up. The last news anchor that he remembered was Walter Cronkite."

•

Peter Boodell works for Flemings U.S., the American division of
the venerable British bank. He remembered attending a party in
Alexi's room one evening. Noticing a large number of books ar-
rayed on the shelves, he asked his host where they were from.

"He replied with the usual 'I was self-taught,' along with some
colorful details of where he studied—some beach or something
as an orphan. I started looking through one, and there was a different person's name inside the cover. I asked him about it (he
was standing right there), since he said they were his books. He
quickly took the book from me and put it back on the bookshelf,
told me it was a used book, and asked me not to look through his
other things."

•

Orin Kerr graduated from the Tower Hill School in Delaware.
His father was a professor at Princeton. "I think the world we live
in is pretty well tracked," he told me when we spoke in Manhattan one afternoon. The world to which he refers is an orderly
place where the graduates of elite schools go on to elite graduate
schools and then to jobs at elite law firms, and become members
of elite clubs. He remembered watching from the bay window of
his room in Holder Hall as Alexi Indris-Santana was tapped for

Ivy, the oldest and most illustrious of Princeton's elite eating clubs and the former haunt of James Baker and Prince Bandar of Saudi Arabia.

"Two guys came and they picked him, and I guess tapped him," Kerr said, using the language that describes the hoped-for culmination of the selection process for the elite clubs, which is known as "bicker"—"and they rushed him out into the courtyard, and poured champagne over his head, and gave him an Ivy hat. And he was screaming and was obviously very excited. And I remember being struck that it was kind of a funny thing, because he really didn't fit the stereotype of someone who would be in Ivy."

A surviving picture of Hogue at the Ivy Club shows a clean-cut young man in a houndstooth jacket, a white button-down shirt, and a silk rep tie. The long hair was gone. His classmates talked about him as a likely candidate for a Rhodes scholarship. With his high grades, his athletic ability, his membership in Ivy, and his remarkable personal story, it was hard to imagine a more likely candidate.

"I think it's tempting to say he's the all-American man," Kerr says with a laugh. "He was living the American Dream, but he took it one step too far. But I think he's really a con man, and that's not a good thing, you know?"

•

Brian Sax is a regional vice president for American Communications Network, a network marketing company in California. He was friends with Santana from the track team, where they were the only two runners with long hair.

"He would deflect any conversation about his past by either asking another question or by saying something totally random. You'd be having a conversation, and the conversation would be going that way, and all of a sudden you'd be talking about something totally different. We'd be talking about track, and if the conversation went in a direction he didn't like, then all of a sudden you'd be talking about Madagascar."

•

Barbi Friedan lives in Princeton. Her manner with adults is fearful, nervous, and almost rabbit-like. She speaks in a soft, high voice that is perfectly pitched for soothing children and reading stories at bedtime. Her husband, Robert Friedan, is a professor of linguistics at Princeton and was Alexi Santana's faculty advisor. He liked Santana because he was less interested in grades than in learning something new. She liked Santana because he was intelligent and shy, and because he was a good influence on her younger son, Bernie, who liked exploring storm drains and engaging in other adventures that frightened his mother. Bernie Friedan worshipped Santana, who had lived on a ranch and slept outdoors, and who told him which storm drains were safe.

Barbi often invited Santana to have dinner at her house in Princeton. On one particularly hot afternoon, she remembered, the air conditioner wasn't working right. Santana got a hose, climbed up on the roof, and sprayed the roof with water to bring the temperature down. He stayed up there for a very long time. When Barbi Friedan walked outside, she was startled to see the hot summer mist rising in waves off the roof of her house.

VII. Boulder

The barefoot runner from Nevada never seemed to realize his promise as a track star at Princeton. While he ran outstanding times in practice, his performance was hampered by nagging, mysterious ailments that often cropped up a day or two before meets, and which he blamed on the poor training regimens designed by Larry Ellis. There were other members of the tight-knit Princeton track team who shared Santana's individualistic approach to training and the belief that they could run better times on their own. Still, Santana seemed to be hanging back in races where he might have pushed himself harder. While his performance improved in the spring of his freshman year, he kept pulling up lame before big races against other Ivy League universities, where lots of fans and reporters were likely to attend.

Brian Sax, the other runner on the team with long hair, understood Santana's behavior as an expression of his hatred for authority and his refusal to obey anyone else's rules. An outsider himself, a native of Southern California with a taste for heavy metal music that the rest of the track team barely tolerated, Sax was struck by Santana's low-key but unrelenting disdain for Ellis, the other track coaches, and his professors. When his coaches told him to walk to one side of the track at a meet, Santana crossed the track, walked over to a nearby fence, and refused to race—just to show that he could, Sax believed. In a geology class that he and Sax took together, Santana flatly refused to redo an assignment. Even more striking than Santana's defiance was the absence of any consequences for his behavior. "They knew his background and they knew how exceptional this person was, so they cut him slack," Sax remembered. "It was Alexi versus authority at Princeton, and Alexi won."

Alexi Santana was special. Everyone on campus knew his story. If his performance on the track left something to be desired, the self-educated runner from Nevada was doing spectacularly well in his classes—earning straight As his first year. The fact that the consummate outsider was adjusting so well to social and academic life made students, teachers, and administrators alike feel good about themselves and their place at an elite institution of higher education whose reputation rests as much on its hoary history of servicing the children of the American elite as it does on the work of the world-class scholars who are chosen to teach there. Sax studied his teammate's behavior carefully, in order to better understand the *Alice in Wonderland* environment in which they found themselves, where the rich and privileged enjoyed the fruits of their family trees while insisting that whatever they had was the result of inborn talent. In their minds, Sax believed, the fact that someone like Alexi Santana was accepted at Princeton was proof of what kind of place Princeton really was. "Alexi had nothing to do with any of these people," Sax explained. "He never went to high school, he had a really tough time growing up, and yet he was a brilliant, brilliant guy. I'm sure the people there felt very, very good that they took Alexi in and nurtured him. I think they thought they might have been instrumental in nurturing him into the brilliant phenom that he so clearly was."

Santana was the answer to skeptics who might portray Princeton as the cloistered preserve of a few thousand rich kids and their big-name tutors. No one wanted to break the spell by giving him an F on an assignment or kicking him off the track team. The character of Alexi Santana had become larger than life. His story was so unusual, and so striking, that it was impossible for him to stay out of the limelight. Mumbling, and answering questions with the fewest possible number of words, he only encouraged his classmates to project their own fantasies of personal achievement and exotic lifestyles onto him. By refusing to run, he only defined himself as a rebel. Isolating himself socially, he heightened the glamour of his outsider origins.

Standing out at Princeton only heightened Santana's fear that something he said or did might give him away. But the impostor was up to the challenge. "One of the things he was really capable of was finding out what made you tick," recalled Jon Luff, who became Santana's best friend on the track team during his freshman year. "He found out what subjects you were interested in, and what your goals were in athletics or beyond college. And then he would play off whatever you told him by telling stories about having done some of those things himself, not necessarily in a competitive way, but not in a particularly modest way, either." When Luff was trying to learn French, his friend began carrying around the works of Voltaire and Rousseau in the original, while modestly denying any special expertise in the language. French was easy to learn, he told Luff. It was something he had picked up along the way. For a granola-eating child of the sixties counterculture who grew up in Santa Cruz and Berkeley, the Nevada desert, and places in between, Luff noticed, Santana also showed an unusual interest in Italian *Vogue,* which he appeared to read voraciously and left lying around his room.

Santana also told Luff stories about training with really good Kenyan runners, who were the stars of the famous University of Texas at El Paso track teams of the late 1970s. He said that he had met the Kenyans while running in Boulder, Colorado, which happened to be Luff's favorite place in the world. As they ran together on the roads outside of Princeton in the morning, he would share his memories of the Kenyans with Luff. "Those guys were great and I loved training with them," he would tell Luff, before segueing into memories of running on the mountain trails

outside Boulder. Alone at Princeton, Luff was glad to find someone who shared his memories of early morning runs in the Rockies, and who loved running as much as he did.

In addition to being a runner, Luff also loved racing bikes, and
knew everything about the latest models from Europe and California. One day, during the Tour de France, when Luff's excitement about bike racing was at its peak, his friend showed up at
his door with a gorgeous new high-end bike that had been spray-
painted black and had no decals or other clues as to its origins.
Santana claimed to have built the bike himself at the Engineering Quad. "He said he made it by himself in about three weeks,
which if you know anything about the difficulty of setting angles
on a bike frame is basically impossible," Luff remembered. To
pull off such a feat, his friend would have needed years of experience and access to highly specialized tools. Still, it was hard not
to give him the benefit of the doubt. Santana did know a great
deal about high-end racing bikes. And there was a sense in which
his stories were simply too good *not* to be true. The special qualities that they saw in this unusual outsider might reside in them,
too. "You wanted to believe in this great character who could just
do anything, and who had created this wonderful life out of nothing," Luff said, years later. "You wanted to believe that this person could exist. So we believed. 'Yeah, he built this bike.' "

As often happened with the stories about Santana that traveled around campus, the legend grew from there. Not only had
Alexi built a world-class racing bike himself from scratch, he was
also a world-class cyclist. Soon, it seemed like everyone knew
that Santana could have been a pro, and was being seriously considered for the Olympics. "That was his method," Luff observed.
"He would plant a little seed, and let the story grow." Everyone
who heard stories about Santana and passed them became a part
of the imposture, but only one person on campus knew for sure
whether or not the stories were true. When Santana was asked

directly about the reports that circulated about his many talents, he usually smiled and shrugged. "It was absolutely fascinating when you look back on it," Luff said. "It's like Jerzy Kosinski's novel *Being There*. By being quiet and saying nothing you become this great person, just because people project their hopes and dreams onto you. And that's exactly what he did, you know?"

In some ways, Santana's second year at Princeton was even more cloistered and private than his first. He stuck close to the Ivy Club, and to his single dorm room. All he remembered about his living quarters that year was a girl named Miriam who lived across the hall. "It was kind of strange, because it had this little bay window, and that was half the room," Santana's creator told me later, remembering the room across the hall, the memory of which had for some reason stayed with him. Miriam had a Georgia O'Keeffe poster on her ceiling, and she played the flute. His other neighbor was a computer major who kept strange hours. Having passed through the promiscuous meeting and greeting of freshman year at an Ivy League college, Santana might stay safe within a close circle of teammates and club members whose familiarity with his story was unlikely to lead to any more questions. He was at home at Princeton but not yet home free.

While distinguished commentators will continue to celebrate the pleasing thought that anyone can strike it rich in America, the graduates of Ivy League colleges know that the competition is hardly equal. The famous names on Ivy League diplomas are backed by the combined weight of the famous men and socially prominent families who have attended Princeton and its brother and sister institutions before. A diploma from Harvard, Princeton, or Yale is a familiar type of social passport, proof that the bearer has been chosen for a place among the elite. The odd doublespeak that surrounds our secular meritocratic version of chosenness has been at once confusing and heartening to generations of undergraduates who have had their individual merits affirmed by the closest thing that the American meritocracy has to the old Puritan idea of election. Yet the power of the old idea was precisely that the choice belonged to God alone, which meant that even the most visibly elect members of society must tremble before the abyss. However odd the Puritan idea of the relationship between God's will and individual destiny might be, it does seem more democratic and less damaging to the social fabric as well as to the lives of individuals than the ritual of gracing a select group of eighteen-year-olds with a place among the elite, the right to preferential treatment in professional school admissions and hiring, and a lifelong network of friends and acquaintances who might help to ease their way along whatever path they might choose to follow.

While most Americans would acknowledge that a Princeton degree is a good thing to have, we rarely talk about why that is so, in large part because the answer is so obvious. Yes, it is a fact that the assurance of being among the elect does not necessarily correspond with actual achievement and can lead to lifelong procrastination and loafing, just as it is a fact that the ranks of authentic American geniuses are filled with people who never went to college.

Still, it is hard to avoid the disorienting, sideways perception that the fluke of my admission to Harvard and then to Princeton is responsible for whatever I may have achieved. The idea that I would always be assured a shot at accomplishing whatever I wanted was hardly prevalent in my upbringing. Without the assurance conferred by my Ivy League acceptance letters, I would have happily copied what other first-generation American children around me did and become an accountant or a lawyer. Yes, there is something narcissistic and ultimately quite delusional about imagining how mediocre your life would be if not for the stroke of good fortune that guarantees that you will walk forever on the sunny side of the street. Fate laughs at pretenses like these, before it decides on the appropriate punishment—cancer, an autistic child, a cheating wife, or getting run over by an ice cream truck. Yet the appeal of the what-if game is undeniably strong for anyone who grows up on the margins of American Life and is gifted with a place at an Ivy League college. In a wink, one's unlucky prior history is erased, to be replaced by the generic things that people think when you say the words "Harvard" or "Princeton" or "Yale"—social refinement, academic achievement, famous novels, political leadership, the pleasures and pretensions of elitist snobbery, and the truly fantastic combination of all of the above, which can finally add up to a sense of belonging to something larger than oneself, whose centrality in the greater American narrative cannot be denied.

In a meritocratic society, acceptance to a university like Princeton is not simply a validation of the person you were when you applied. Rather, it means that you are free to become someone new. In turn, the university will testify to the social legitimacy of your actions by putting its name on your diploma. Your troubled or unworthy old self can be safely discarded in favor of the aura conferred by the institution and by the collective achievements of its well-placed graduates around the globe. Later on, if you wish, you can reveal yourself as you are, or were, and share the embarrassing details of your origins and upbringing—that is to say, of the person you were before you acquired a proper education and a dresser full of Scottish cashmere sweaters, and learned to comport yourself as a member of the elite whose first lie is that that there is no such thing as an elite in America.

That James Hogue was puzzled by the magical nature of this exchange, which arrogates to a small number of universities the power to erase the past, and turn dross into gold, is not surprising. Focused on the success of his own con, it seems fair to say that he understood Princeton's unwritten contract with its students only in part. Here and there, in our conversations, which were pieced together over a period of months, his sense of bewilderment shows through, in a way that made me feel sorry for him every time I read the transcripts. There were thirteen tapes in all. Each of the tapes lasted from forty-five minutes to one hour long, and was filled with long pauses, which suggest that the Princeton con man was also a naif.

"I can remember specific little things, like the guy who was showing me around," he told me, speaking of Jon Luff. "He had a rack with forty ties on it in his room. I was thinking to myself, why does a college student need forty ties? Where is he wearing these ties? Or the first time I visited here it was cold and raining, and I was thinking, 'Bloody hell, it's going to snow. This is pretty awful weather. I haven't seen rain in a long, long time. Is it like this a lot? Why can I go into the library, and they have three million volumes and they don't have a single book on pediatrics?' It just seemed kind of absurd to me. You could go into any public library in the United States, no matter how small, and they would have at least one book about pediatrics."

Extrapolate from details like these, Hogue instructed me, and I would understand how he felt about Princeton. There were gaps in the story that Princeton was trying to tell about itself. The desire to distinguish yourself from the herd is inherent in human nature. Because we don't have a caste system to tell us who is better and worse than everyone else, we ask people we meet where they went to college.

"I don't think in any other country people would put a sticker in the back window of their car about where they went to college," Hogue earnestly explained to me. "I don't know if that's any different than somebody that wears a baseball cap that says

Caterpillar as opposed to John Deere or something," he continued. We were sitting around the fire someplace that he would
rather not talk about. "I mean, what are they trying to say? That
they're better because they're wearing John Deere, you know?"
He felt guilty about lying to people, he says, but not guilty
enough to stop. I don't believe he felt guilty at all.

There were differences in our situations, of course. I never
risked going to jail. Still, I knew what it felt like to wonder about
the number of ties in my roommate's closet. Accepting my ticket
to an Ivy League college made me a willing participant in the
greater fraud of a meritocracy in which some were ordained
more equal than others. I knew very well at eighteen that there
was no shortage of unfairness to go around. I was grateful for
the chance to escape the life that had been chosen for me by
my parents and teachers, who wanted me to live according to
strict rules that they believed were part of the divine order of
things—not turning on lights on the Sabbath or waiting six hours
to drink milk after eating meat—which seemed to me like symptoms of collective mental derangement, rather than true expres-
sions of God's Plan. The possibility that I was right and my
parents and teachers were wrong, a possibility that I held on to
for years against the combined force of authority at home and
at school and contrary to the tugs of affection and affiliation that
I felt in my own heart, was finally and irrefutably confirmed on
the day that I received my Harvard acceptance letter in the mail.
On that day, the dark clouds of obedience parted and a heavenly
finger reached out and touched my forehead. I was transformed
into a living, breathing person, an individual with the God-given
right to be whoever I wanted to be. If the price of this precious
gift was the betrayal of everything that I had been before, will-
ingly or unwillingly, so be it. I was happy to shed my skin and
assume a new identity backed by the precious piece of paper

that certified me as a plausible member of the elite. Hogue's story had an added twist. He was a ghost who became a living, breathing vessel for his own myths and dreams, and for the myths and dreams of others. And when it was over, he went back to being a ghost.

VIII. The Recognition

On February 16, 1991, a senior at Yale named Renee Pacheco attended the Harvard-Yale-Princeton track meet in New Haven to watch a friend run, and she noticed that one of the members of the Princeton team looked familiar. Their eyes met, and she recognized Jay Mitchell Huntsman, a mysterious stranger who had arrived at Palo Alto High School in September 1985.

Jay Huntsman, or Riivk, as he called himself, was a talented runner who had arrived at her school with an incredible story. He was born in San Diego in 1969, and had moved at the age of eight to Ananda Ashram, a Nevada commune where he lived with his parents, Craig and Rosemary Huntsman, and his sister, Solange. He had educated himself. During the breaks in his work, he ran between fifty and sixty miles a week, and after his parents died in a car accident in Bolivia, he had decided to attend Palo Alto High School to complete his education before applying to Stanford University. He found a room in town. He made friends at school. Parents liked him.

A few weeks after Huntsman appeared in Palo Alto, he entered the Stanford Invitational meet. Blowing past the rest of the field, he won the cross-country race, but he never reported to the officials' table. He had trained in the wide-open spaces of Nevada, he told a reporter for the *Mercury News*. "I'm just a normal kid," he added. "I just want to fit in."

Some of the reporters who watched the race found it troubling that the "mystery runner," as the local papers soon dubbed him, had failed to claim his victory. Acting on a hunch, Jason Cole, a reporter with a Palo Alto newspaper, the *Peninsula Times Tribune,* called the municipal office in charge of public records for the city of San Diego and asked if there was a birth certificate on file for a Jay Mitchell Huntsman. There was. Born to Craig and Rosemary Huntsman of 3145 Rosecranz Place, in San Diego, on January 19, 1969, Jay Mitchell Huntsman had died two days later of pneumonia. Cole told the school authorities about his discovery and reported it in the *Times Tribune*. The student soon acknowledged that his real name was James Hogue, and left town after passing a bad check.

After seeing Hogue at the Princeton-Yale track meet, Pacheco called Paul Jones, the coach of the track team at Palo Alto High, who put her in touch with Jason Cole. "I saw him running," Pacheco told Cole. "I walked right up to him—I'm surprised he didn't recognize me. I just wanted to scream."

Pacheco didn't scream. But she was sure that Alexi Santana and James Hogue were the same person. Her father was a professor at Stanford, and she had not enjoyed the experience of being fooled by Hogue, who had eased his way into the company of the upper-class professionals of Palo Alto by flattering their self-image as caring, open-minded people who worked hard and eminently deserved the good life they enjoyed.

Cole knew that the administrators and students of Princeton University were about to experience a similar shock. After finding out that Hogue had been arrested in Utah, the reporter contacted the police to inform them of Hogue's whereabouts. Then he informed Princeton that Alexi Santana was actually James Hogue, an ex-convict from Utah who had jumped his parole and had engaged in similar deceptions before. "We know you don't know this about your undergraduate, but he's a phony," Cole told Princeton. "You guys might want to be thinking about what you want to say publicly, because I can pretty much predict that this is going to be a big story."

Justin Harmon, director of communications at Princeton, was grateful for the warning. He got off the phone, and he phoned one of the deans of the college, who called a meeting with Dean of Admissions Fred Hargadon and several of his colleagues in order to decide on how the university should respond. Santana's file was produced. His application, with his essay about working on a ranch in Nevada and learning to read Plato under the stars, was reviewed again. Taking six or seven courses a semester, Santana had received a grade of A in nearly every class he took for almost two years. Attention was also paid to the university's role as a custodian of public funds. "It became clear to us," Harmon remembered, "particularly to the deans, that the only course of action, from the standpoint of the institution, since this young man had applied to Princeton under utterly false pretenses, was to declare the admission null and void."

Alexi Santana was a phantom, summoned forth by an imaginative drifter from Utah with a flair for telling people at places like Princeton the kinds of stories they wanted to hear. Now that the truth was known, the face of the phantom student would dissolve into that of his creator, the ex-con. Since Hogue had been admitted to Princeton under false pretenses, the records of his time at the university were also false. By the time the meeting was over, the Princeton deans had agreed on a course of action: Alexi Santana, member of the Class of 1993, was officially expunged from the university's records. It was like he had never really existed at all.

IX. The Fall

The problem of James Hogue's physical presence on the Princeton campus took less than twenty-four hours to solve. On Tuesday, February 26, two men in suits arrived at the door of the laboratory classroom where John Suppe was teaching Geology 316, a class that dealt with large-scale structural phenomena such as faulting and folding that are associated with violent ruptures in the surface of the earth.

Brian Sax was one of eight students in the classroom that afternoon. It was an interesting class, he remembered. It interested him enough that, almost ten years later, he could still remember the subject in exacting detail. "We were given all the stresses and strains put on a well due to all the faults in a general area," he said. "When you've got a well, usually it's perfectly cylindrical. But then, after time, it deforms. Sometimes," he continued, after a longer, more technical explanation of the pressures that might affect the well, "it will get more oval-shaped, and so you know that there are pressures coming in from different directions and different layers of rock."

The men at the door were not interested in shifting plates or geological stresses. They took the professor aside and told him that they needed to speak with one of his students. Santana joined the two men outside, and they asked him his name. His answer, "James Hogue," was not audible to the rest of the students in the room. "All of a sudden they started reading him his rights, and they put him in cuffs right there," Sax remembered. "And we said, 'Holy shit! What's going on?' "

As news of the arrest spread around campus, about fifteen to twenty members of the track team gathered in Jon Luff's room, which was in one of the older dorms on campus, with wood floors and an open fireplace—the perfect admissions brochure picture of what a dorm room looks like at Princeton. When Sax entered the room, Luff was on the phone with Jason Cole in California. The atmosphere reminded Sax of the silence that follows an upset in sports. The phone kept ringing. With each phone call new bits and pieces of information about their teammate filtered in. He had been arrested for stealing bicycles in Utah. He had served time in prison. He had been to college before.

"There was an air of total disbelief," Sax remembered. "There were no words for what had happened, because here was somebody who was a good friend of a lot of people in the room and all of a sudden he's somebody totally different. And we know very, very little about this person, and he could possibly be dangerous. People were saying, 'What did he do? Did he commit murder? Did he commit multiple felonies?' "

Luff, who had spent the previous summer living with Santana in Boulder, Colorado, and knew him better than anyone else on the team, appeared to be in shock. The shy young man he had shown around Princeton was not twenty years old. He was thirty-two. Now that he knew that Alexi Santana was an impostor named James Hogue, the gaps in his friend's stories, and some of his odd behavior, began to make sense. The racing bike that he supposedly built from scratch had been stolen from Dave Tesch's shop. The African runners he had run against, like Joseph Nzau, who were famous when Santana would have been fourteen years old, were real people, figures from Hogue's past.

Santana's creator possessed an undeniable genius, Luff believed. At the same time, he felt betrayed by the fact that his friend had turned out to be someone else. The troubling encounter with a person who was actually someone else haunted Luff for many years thereafter. As he racked his brain in search of clues to the mystery of who James Hogue was, and what he was

actually like, he returned again and again to the summer between his freshman and sophomore year. He couldn't remember
exactly how Santana came to live in the house that he shared with
his older brother in Boulder that summer. Santana had crashed
on the couch one night, and somehow never left. As the summer
wore on, Luff had become progressively less enchanted with his
new roommate. Santana stayed up late at night, and rummaged
through closets and cupboards. Luff and his roommates began to
notice that food and personal items, like CDs, jackets, and
money, were missing. While Santana claimed to have a job at a
local ski shop refurbishing skis, he slept all day and never left the
house. When the roommates gathered for dinner, he would talk
about his job as if he had worked a full day. One of the roommates determined that the ski shop at which Santana claimed to
work never existed. But perhaps he was mistaken. Santana also
told stories about outracing famous runners that Luff knew personally. Luff knew at the time that the stories were lies. Santana
also claimed to have entered local races and run remarkably fast
times. Luff found these stories particularly baffling because he
was working that summer in the sports department of a local
newspaper, and had easy access to the official results of the races
that Santana claimed to have run, and in which his friend's name
never appeared.

Still, Santana's brand of weirdness was hardly that unusual
among the world-class athletes who congregated in Boulder during the summers, running lonely marathons in the mountains
late at night in search of a jolt of transcendence and then sleeping
through their day jobs. The two runners from Princeton continued their friendship for most of the summer. A frequent subject
of conversation was their classmate Peter Hessler, who often
spoke of his hope of winning a Rhodes scholarship. Santana was
fascinated by Hessler's ambition, and he decided that he would
give the Rhodes scholarship a shot, too. He would keep up his

grades and continue to run track. His unique life story and his membership in the Ivy Club would impress the Rhodes selection committee. Luff agreed that Santana's goal was certainly plausible.

Since Santana was an accomplished outdoorsman, Luff was eager to take him camping in the San Juan Mountains in Colorado with his friends from high school, who were also in Boulder that summer. "It was one of those classic American camping trips, where you go out in the woods or the mountains with your two best friends to the same place you've been five times since you were kid," Luff recalled. His friends liked to drink, and were annoyed when Santana refused the beer that they had lugged up the side of a mountain. When the three childhood friends climbed a mountain peak together one day and slept in the next morning, Santana decided to go running. He returned to the campsite two hours later and told Luff that he had run to the top of the neighboring mountain and back on his own—a feat that would have taken an experienced climber the better part of a day. Luff's friends were not impressed. "They were just like, 'This guy is so full of shit,' " Luff ruefully remembered. " 'I can't believe that you're even friends with this guy, Jon.' "

Plenty of Princeton students have had the experience of having friends from back home take an instant dislike to their college friends, who seem snobbish or pretentious or otherwise annoying, and who threaten the familiar rhythms of childhood friendship. But his friends' visceral dislike of Santana took Luff by surprise. The climax of the trip came when the three friends and Luff's new friend from college neared the spectacular peak of Wetterhorn, one of the jewels of the San Juan Mountains. Before they reached the top of the mountain, the trail ended, leaving fifty feet of broken rock between the climbers and the peak. It was a difficult passage, but nothing that would make an experienced climber sweat. "If you looked in the guidebook it said,

'Ropes aren't required, but suggested,' " Luff recalled. "And we were like, 'No, forget that. We'll just scramble to the top.' "

When he looked over at Santana, Luff saw that his friend appeared to be paralyzed with fear. "He was absolutely petrified, so shaky that we didn't think we could get him to the peak," Luff remembered. "And all three of us were just sort of standing around for a while, wondering, 'This guy is supposed to be a rugged outdoorsman who spent his whole life in the mountains and running barefoot through desert canyons and now he can't make it up this semi-exposed little staircase of rock.' " As the four climbers began their descent, a sudden bolt of lighting hit near the top of the mountain. While lightning storms are common in the Rockies during the summer, Santana again seemed terrified, and refused to move from where he was standing. "For a while, I think we thought he was joking," Luff said. "But he was truly petrified. And we were like, 'This guy supposedly lived his life outdoors, herding cattle on five-thousand-foot-high plateaus in Utah, and now he's afraid of a lightning storm.' You get lightning storms every afternoon in Utah and Colorado. But he was clearly not comfortable, and it just seemed odd."

James Hogue was held at the Princeton Township police station on Nassau Street, just outside the university gates. He was interviewed there by Lieutenant John Redding, who remembered that Hogue appeared sad but composed, and that he readily answered whatever questions he was asked.

Q: Can you explain why you have done this twice—you have reported to be someone you're not?

A: I didn't feel that I learned what I wanted to learn, and I wanted to go back to college.

Q: Under what name did you apply to Princeton University?

A: Under Alexi Santana.

Q: Where did you obtain that name?

A: I made that up.

Q: For what purpose?

A: I wanted to start all over again, without the burdens of my past.

In the course of the interview, Lieutenant Redding asked James Hogue exactly one hundred and fifty questions and received exactly one hundred and fifty answers. Under terrible pressure, and facing the collapse of what was both a saving act of self-invention and his greatest con yet, Hogue answered every one of the lieutenant's questions with a polite and deadpan calm, without telling lies and without revealing much of interest about himself or his past. Perhaps the mystery of Alexi Santana was too personal to share with a policeman. Or perhaps the mystery was all he had left.

Hogue's story quickly caught the attention of the national media, but he refused to speak to reporters. Charged with theft by deception and three counts of forgery, and unable to make bail, he was transferred to the Mercer County Correctional Center to await trial. There he received visits from the Friedans, who found him sad but composed and adjusting well to the rigors of prison life, and from Peter Hessler, who hoped to write an article about his friend for *Rolling Stone*. While the article never appeared, Hessler did achieve his dream of becoming a Rhodes Scholar and later wrote an acclaimed book about his experiences teaching English in rural China.

Polly Robbins also visited Hogue in jail. A junior at Princeton, Robbins had grown up on the Upper East Side of Manhattan. Her father ran a small brokerage on Wall Street. Attractive and wealthy, Robbins nonetheless did not fit in with the preppies and outdoor types at Princeton. Santana was gentle, funny, and a catch. In the weeks before his arrest, he had told Robbins that he might have to go back to Utah, but he was vague about exactly why. Santana and Robbins began to talk seriously about leaving Princeton and moving together to the desert. It was all very dramatic, but somehow the conversations never resolved themselves into a clear explanation of why Santana might have to leave. Perhaps he had recognized Renee Pacheco at the Princeton-Yale track meet, just as she had recognized him.

When Hogue was arrested, he asked for permission to call Polly Robbins, who came by around 8 P.M. that same evening. She brought Hogue the key to his dorm room along with his wallet. Inside the wallet, investigators found a copy of a birth certificate made out in the name of "Alexi Indris-Santana," as well as a Selective Service registration card bearing Santana's name. Then she called Pacheco in New Haven and yelled at her for destroying her boyfriend's life.

Polly's father helped find Hogue a lawyer, though as the case became public, and the trial date drew nearer, her parents became ever more eager for the relationship to end. Polly refused to stop seeing Hogue. The Friedans would pick her up in their car and drive her to Trenton. Before she entered the jail, she would stand outside and chain-smoke cigarettes, dressed in black and wearing sunglasses: she was the bad girl with the bad boyfriend.

"I think Alexi was talking about marriage, or something along those lines," remembered Jon Luff, who had lunch with her a number of times during the trial. He remembered that Polly Robbins was unhappy at Princeton and had a hard time socially. Meeting Santana was the best thing that had happened to her at Princeton, she suggested. "I think that really added to the trauma for her, because she was finally happy," Luff said. Confused and upset, Robbins struggled to process the fact that the love of her life was a drifter with a criminal record. "Polly felt like maybe he was trying to tell her that he really did have this life of deception, and that he might have to go back to Utah to finish his jail time there, since he had violated his parole by leaving the state to come to Princeton," Luff remembered. "She told me some stories that suggested that he was trying to convey that information to her. But he wasn't necessarily successful." Polly did know that Santana was afraid that his life at Princeton might end, but she didn't know exactly why—and she never dared to ask. He was too important for her to risk pushing him away.

Robbins' tortured feelings of love and betrayal were shared to some extent by a few other members of the Princeton community who in one way or another had been close to Hogue. Larry Ellis had spent a lifetime compiling an impeccable record as a track coach that was intended in some part as a reproof to those who questioned whether a black man was equipped to coach at the highest levels of his sport. A proud, caring man, and a consummate politician, Ellis had blazed new ground for black coaches in the formerly all-white American track-and-field establishment, using the head coaching job at Princeton as a springboard to coaching the men's Olympic track team and holding other high positions in national track-and-field organizations. As the story of the Princeton impostor continued to make headlines, Ellis found himself in the humiliating position of the dupe. His enthusiasm for the unusual recruit he had treated with such paternal care had contributed to one of the more embarrassing incidents in Princeton University's history.

The jokes from his fellow coaches on the college circuit were even harder for Ellis to handle. Brian Sax recalled that the ribbing went on for the better part of the next year and a half. "How about that Alexi?" rival coaches would ask, remarking on how Princeton had been fooled by a homeless drifter. "He'd get this look in his eyes like, 'Oh my God, not this again,' and sort of cower away from them," Sax said, describing Ellis's typical reaction to comments by other coaches about the impostor. Sax and others observed that Ellis's hurt over the incident appeared to linger long after the comments stopped.

Opinion among students and faculty at Princeton seemed evenly divided between those who thought that the impostor was guilty of very little besides the desire to get a good education, and those who saw him as a criminal and were glad that he was gone. For many, the fact that a homeless drifter had fooled the Princeton admissions office with a tall tale about running barefoot in the desert canyons and reading Plato under the stars was the occasion for some laughter at their own expense. A homeless drifter could get As at Princeton. For Brian Sax, the joke was as much on Hogue as it was on the Princeton admissions committee and all the people who took his made-up story so seriously. Hogue's own need for approval was so great that he was willing to risk jail time for a piece of paper that he could have obtained legitimately with much less effort from a more low-key university. The idea that other people care all that much about who you are—as opposed to what you can do for them in the next hour or two—is a misconception that is especially common among Ivy League graduates, Sax believed. "Some people feel very, very good when they say, 'Man, I went to Princeton,' and everybody goes, 'Oooooh,' " Sax concluded. "And they're thinking, hey, these people think I'm the man because I went to Princeton, when in reality they just don't give a shit. They don't care at all."

The members of the Ivy Club were particularly nonplussed by the fact that "the funny old man," as they had affectionately nicknamed the newest member of their exclusive social club—no one I spoke with could remember who tagged Santana with such a prescient name—had turned out to be a convicted felon. None of Hogue's friends from the Ivy Club wrote letters on his behalf to the judge who heard his case or visited him in jail. As Tom Pinckney, a fellow Ivy Club member from the Class of 1993, recalled, "I think I thought that Alexi had changed into this guy James Hogue, who I wasn't friends with. I don't know anybody who tried to get in touch with him."

Hogue's most frequent visitor in jail was a Princeton professor named Giancinto Scoles, a gentle man who had been educated in Italy and who taught classes in physical chemistry. Scoles was widely recognized in the scientific community for his work with vacuum beams, or lasers, which he used to solve problems related to the basic structure of matter. He was famous at Princeton for his unorthodox method of determining the final grades that students would receive in his classes. After assigning a final project, Scoles would call his students into his office one by one and ask them what grade they thought they deserved. If the grade was similar to the grade Scoles thought they had earned, they would receive the grade they had assigned themselves. If the grade they suggested was more than one plus or minus removed from the grade Scoles chose, they would have to take a final exam in order to gauge their actual knowledge of the subject. In the class he took with Scoles, Hogue submitted a final project that investigated the thermal dynamics of a children's toy, a bird that dipped its beak in a glass of water. The B+ he received in Scoles's class his freshman year was the only grade less than an A that he received at Princeton. When they met for a counseling session after the class, Scoles suggested that he might want to major in geology.

Scoles saw Hogue as a con man, but one who had a strong sense of intellectual curiosity. Seeing him in prison was a shock. Scoles was bothered by having to get permission in advance, stand in front of the prison gates as they slowly opened, and talk to his former student through a thick sheet of Plexiglas. Hogue wasn't a person who belonged in prison, Scoles concluded. He was a person who needed friendship and psychological help. A friend and colleague at Princeton warned Scoles that cases like Hogue's could not be solved by well-meaning intervention. Past a certain age, the colleague said, people never change—they won't, or they can't.

Scoles disagreed. Hogue, he believed, was simply careless about the consequences of his actions. When he asked Hogue questions about his life, he learned that his student had grown up in a blue-collar family in Kansas, and that he liked running. Although the answers Hogue gave were honest, Scoles saw, they were also strangely detached. It was as if Hogue were answering questions about someone else. To occupy his friend in prison, Scoles gave him a thermodynamics textbook in Italian to translate into English. When he was released from prison before his trial date, Scoles offered him money, which Hogue refused. He also helped him relocate to Cambridge, Massachusetts, where he took classes at the Harvard Extension School and was hired part-time to help curate the university's collection of precious minerals and gems. More than $40,000 worth of minerals and gems, along with an expensive microscope belonging to the university and a chair with the Harvard seal, were later discovered in Hogue's room. Princeton could now enjoy a laugh at Harvard's expense.

Hogue's attorney, Bob Obler, had hoped to put Princeton University on trial before a jury, which might sympathize with the young runner from a poor family who had tried to better himself by seeking an Ivy League education. Instead, on February 10, 1992, his client appeared before Judge Paulette Sapp-Peterson at the Mercer County Courthouse and pled guilty to a charge of theft by deception.

"I submitted an application at Princeton University which had a different name and date of birth," he explained, as he stood before the court in an orange prison jumpsuit, which reminded at least some observers of the Princeton colors, orange and black. "It was my intent to gain admission by deception."

"It was your intent to gain admission by deception," Judge Sapp-Peterson repeated, "and when you say it was your intent to gain admission by deception, your deception occurred by submitting false information on your application?"

"Correct."

"And using a false name?"

"Yes."

In the audience, members of the Princeton track team watched, mouths agape, as their former teammate was sentenced to two hundred and seventy days at the Mercer County Correction Center, one hundred hours of community service, and five years' probation; he was also ordered to make restitution of $21,124 upon his release. Stories about the Princeton impostor duly appeared in *People, Sports Illustrated,* the *New York Times,* the *Washington Post,* and various other national and local publications. "He was average, I guess," Hogue's father Eugene Hogue told the *Philadelphia Inquirer.* "I don't have any idea why it would happen."

For Justin Harmon, the peppy university spokesman who spent months handling gleeful press inquiries about how Princeton had been fooled, Alexi Santana remained a terrific candidate for admission, "a very bright, imaginative young man who appeared to have a hunger for learning and a willingness to pursue learning energetically, and who had, over the course of his life's experiences, faced a number of circumstances that kids don't commonly face, from the experience on the ranch to his travels in Europe, to his relationship with his mother in Switzerland—I believe that was the story—to the books that he'd read, to his way of describing the books." Santana was a model applicant in every respect, except for the fact that he was a fictional character.

The idea of allowing Santana's creator to proceed with his studies never crossed anyone's mind. Allowing Hogue to stay at Princeton would have been a serious breach of the university's responsibility to other applicants and to U.S. taxpayers, whose contributions help fund wealthy private universities that sit on multibillion-dollar endowments while using public moneys to build dorms and pay for scientific equipment and to fund an admissions process that actively discriminates in favor of their own alumni.

"The fact is that alumni children do have a better chance than the average kid of getting in," Harmon explained to me in a subsequent interview. "There's a sense of tradition about the thing." I asked him why Princeton continues to favor the children of alumni while accepting hundreds of millions of dollars a year in public money.

"That's a good question," he answered. "There's a sense on the part of the school that they're from families who know the institution well, are familiar with the faculty, who do interviewing for us, who help raise money, who set up programs for students to help them find jobs, and so it's a factor in the admissions process. There are no two ways about it." When I mentioned that the children of alumni at Harvard and Princeton had SAT scores that were 150 points lower on average than the children of non-alumni, Harmon didn't exactly disagree. "I think it's dangerous to focus an assessment of the relative strength of various applications on a number like SAT scores," he purred. "We admit kids with much better scores and much lower scores."

The children of alumni, it turns out, have experiences and talents that cannot be reduced to a crude number, like an SAT score. I suggested to Harmon that many kids with low scores who are admitted to Princeton are minority candidates who come from backgrounds that are defined as economically or culturally deprived. I asked Harmon whether being the child of a Princeton alumnus also qualified as a form of deprivation, like growing up poor in inner-city Cleveland.

"No," the Princeton spokesman answered, adding again that SAT scores are an imperfect gauge of a student's ability. As he explained that the wording of questions of the SAT could reflect cultural biases that could lead to lesser scores for certain groups, it seemed plain to me that there was something terribly warped in the conjunction of Princeton's old-boy network and textbook socially progressive attitudes espoused by the admissions committee: in the university's own mind, it seemed, discrimination in favor of one class of candidates gave Princeton a free pass to discriminate in favor of the children of its own alumni.

"Certainly, none of these arguments apply to alumni children, who tend to be by and large economically advantaged and have had good school experiences," Harmon admitted, when I suggested that there was something disgusting about using the same arguments intended to help poor black kids from the inner city in order to favor the children of the most wealthy and privileged members of American society. "It's an article of faith in American higher education that having a class that represents a broad array of experiences and backgrounds is a good thing."

Hogue's application to Princeton may have started out as a prank, or as a calculated con, or as the heartfelt dream of a lonely young man who was eager to change the circumstances of his life and leave his checkered past behind him. When it became public, it became part of a large referendum on the self-appointed, self-described meritocracy that presented itself as the new and hopeful face of a forward-looking America. The country's meritocrat-in-chief at the time was Bill Clinton, a poor boy from Arkansas whose father had left home when he was two years old, and who survived an abusive stepfather to make it to Georgetown, Oxford, and Yale, and then became the president of the

United States. If education remained a way that the children of the poor and low-born might achieve success in America, the meritocratic system was also in some part a fraud that existed to perpetuate the privileges of the wealthy. As such, the college admissions system that guarded the doors to America's elite universities became a magnet for frauds, who invented new histories for themselves in order to achieve the social benefits and class distinction that an Ivy League degree might confer. There was Lon Grammer, the Yale transfer student with a straight-A transcript and a colorful career as a minor league baseball player who was unmasked six weeks before graduation as a C student from Cuesta Community College in California; he had forged a new transcript and written his recommendation letters himself. "I definitely feel I belonged," an unrepentant Grammer told the *New York Times,* adding, perhaps ungraciously, "I've met lugheads there."

At Duke, Maurice de Rothschild made a splash throwing lavish benefit parties for the swim team and purchasing bunches of *Gloriosa rothschildana,* the Rothschild lily, from Campus Florist in Durham; his career as a campus Rothschild ended when he was eventually revealed to be Mauro Cortez Jr., the thirty-seven-year-old son of Mexican migrants who lived in El Paso. Gina Grant's story was perhaps the best known. Applying for admission under her own name, she was admitted to Harvard, which then revoked its offer once it found out that she had bludgeoned her mother to death with a lead crystal candlestick, a detail that might have been lifted from a gothic novel.

Beneath the old-fashioned, black-and-white phrases— "fraud," "con artist," "impostor" —that were used to describe the offenders in these and other publicized cases of successful imposture at America's elite colleges and universities, it was possible to feel a very unreportorial anger at work. The *New Republic* denounced "upwardly mobile delinquents and professional wild children," whose hankering for advancement and degenerate interest in wild partying set them miles apart from the magazine's sober-minded editors, who studied hard and were often the products of distinguished families. The Lon Grammer case led editorialists at the *Yale Daily News* and the *New York Times* to question the integrity of the elite college admissions process, which routinely asked tens of thousands of high school seniors to twist themselves into odd shapes and take on meaningless extracurricular activities in order to satisfy the weird social and class preferences of admissions officers and alumni. "[We] were . . . impressed to know what it would be like to be or know a Rothschild," assistant dean Paul Bumbalough of Duke admitted to a reporter to *Rolling Stone,* by way of explaining why admissions officers, faculty, and students at Duke did not notice that the Rothschild among them couldn't speak French.

The angry denunciations of "frauds" and "impostors" on university campuses neatly avoided any examination of the increasing importance of credentials obtained at the age of eighteen with the help of elite coaching and well-connected parents, and tended to obscure rather than reveal the sources of what was, after all, the defining American act. As a nation, America had created itself through a collective act of self-invention, rebelling against the English colonial government and asserting the right to self-determination of a people that had no prior existence in history or law. Enshrined in the Constitution, the freedom to create one's own individual identity had defined American literature since its beginnings in the *Autobiography of Benjamin Franklin,* the story of the poor printer's apprentice who had scrimped and saved to become one of the richest men in the thirteen colonies. That Franklin's autobiography was riddled with lies only underlined the truth of its author's assertion that Americans would be free to invent themselves in whatever image they chose, transcending the established boundaries of history, tradition, race, creed, gender, and class to become self-invented women or men. A partial list of Americans who invented themselves in this fashion would include P.T. Barnum, Thomas Alva Edison, John D. Rockefeller, Andrew Carnegie, Clark Gable, Bob Dylan, Jimi Hendrix, Madonna, Jay-Z, and Eminem, as well as millions of other immigrants, inventors, writers, preachers, shouters, movie stars, bankers, thieves, cranks, gurus, promotional wizards, mountebanks, rap artists, and American presidents from Washington and Andrew Jackson to Ronald Reagan, Bill Clinton, and George W. Bush. The major theme of American lives, self-invention and the lies that people tell when making themselves up from scratch is also a subject of most great American novels, from Melville's *The Confidence Man* to *The Adventures of Huckleberry Finn, The Great Gatsby, The Adventures of Augie March,* and *The Invisible Man.* The darkness present in these stories is not always acknowledged by their protagonists, their readers or, for that matter, their authors. Still, it is there.

James Hogue returned from Cambridge to New Jersey for his sentencing on December 18, 1992, and served five months. The same day that he was released, he was arrested for the theft of the gems. His time in jail was uneventful, his cell mate Donald Salentre Jr. remembered. He kept to himself. "It looked like he was in his own little world. He wasn't in jail." Salentre said that Hogue would sit on the top bunk of their two-person cell, put a blanket over his head, and read, losing himself in the highly abstract universe of *Life in Moving Fluids* and other books about engineering, mechanics, and physics. Another favorite book was *Mineral Lands and Mining.* He told Salentre that he hoped to stake a claim to mining lands out west when he got out of jail: he served an additional seventeen month jail sentence in Utah for violating his parole and the theft of the gems. And then, once more, he disappeared.

X. The Bicycle Thief

On the evening of July 15, 1997, Officer Jeff Harmon of the Aspen police department took a complaint from a man named Michael Otte about the theft of a Schwinn bicycle. Officer Harmon remembered seeing a similar bicycle the night before, locked to a tree by the Hyman Avenue pedestrian mall. The next evening, Harmon and his partner, Vicki Nall, found the stolen bicycle, locked to a tree in the same area. James Hogue was working the lock.

"Police! You're under arrest!" Nall shouted. Hogue shoved her backward, turned around, and ran into Harmon. Nall handcuffed him and took him to the Pitkin County jail. Hogue's arrest and subsequent conviction, on a second charge of bicycle theft, became part of the Pitkin County records and eventually led me to his address.

I had discovered many interesting facts about the life of James Hogue. He was born in Wyandotte County, Kansas, in 1959. I had visited the house where he grew up—a small, single-story ranch house in a working-class neighborhood of Kansas City, Kansas. I had spoken to classmates of his from high school in Wyandotte County and from his college years, which were spent in Laramie, Wyoming, and Austin, Texas. I was particularly interested in the relationship between Hogue and the character he had created. Santana, it seemed to me, had balanced out the parts of Hogue that were unstable and weak and most in need of protection. Now that protection was gone. Hogue moved from rented room to rented room in the mountain resort towns of Colorado. He spent some time in Telluride, where he did construction work. Once I felt sure about the outlines of his actual life story, I mailed a package to a post office box in Aspen containing a videotape and a letter that expressed my desire to learn more. When he didn't answer, I went to find him. He left Aspen shortly before I arrived.

The videotape I sent contained a few brief segments of interviews I had conducted with people Hogue had known while growing up in Kansas. Among the segments on the tape was a long conversation I had with Keith Mark, a labor lawyer from Kansas City whose bowl-cut hair increases his already strong resemblance to his boyhood hero, Pete Rose.

Like Hogue, Mark grew up in Wyandotte County, ran track at Washington High School, and had a father who worked for the railroad. Hogue had been his closest friend. When Hogue went to McDonald's, Mark remembered, he always ordered a Big Mac without the burger. He slept on the floor in a sleeping bag and read running magazines. He ran with bells on his feet so that he would be more aware of the rhythm of his stride. Photographs of Hogue running show a lean, movie-star-handsome kid who holds himself with the easy confidence of a champion. In many of the photographs, Hogue is wearing dark aviator-framed sunglasses, to make it harder for competitors to read him.

Running, Mark explained, was a ticket out. It was a chance to follow in the footsteps of famous Kansas milers like Glenn Cunningham and Jim Ryun, and to win an athletic scholarship to college. Hogue excelled in school, where he did well in chemistry and mathematics, and read *The Catcher in the Rye* and *Rabbit, Run.* He liked to listen to his mother's classical records, but he ran to rock and roll. He would run to anything from Ted Nugent to REO Speedwagon to Boston. The two runners swapped songs that might inspire them to run farther and faster. For a while, Keith Mark remembered, Hogue was hooked on the trashy Jefferson Airplane pop song "Miracles." He got so lost in the song that he ran on and on with the floating chorus "If only you believe like I believe, baby/We'd get by" repeating in his head before he realized that he was fifteen miles away from where he had started.

Hogue liked making an impression on people, Mark remembered. He set his watch in synch with the Master Clock at the Naval Observatory in Colorado Springs. At parties, he might bum a cigarette, so that people would say, "Oh man, that's Jim Hogue smoking, how does he do that?"—even though he didn't really smoke. He didn't wear his letter jacket in the glass-walled breezeway where the other athletes hung out between classes at Washington High so everyone could see how cool they were. He didn't need the cheerleaders coming up to him and saying, "Oh, you're Jim Hogue." After Jim won a BlueCross BlueShield Road Race in Kansas City, he was running back with Keith Mark to his car, and the two runners passed a lady standing on the corner with a little kid who was bawling his eyes out. "Jim said, 'Hey, stop crying,' " Keith Mark remembered. "And he gives the kid his plaque or his medal, man. Never missed a beat. He just kept on going."

Hogue never seemed to care about the medals he won. But making a good impression was important to him. When Hogue won a race, he would go out to his father's car and change his clothes. When the announcer called his name after the race, he would step up to the podium to accept his medal, neatly attired in slacks and a dress shirt. At a meet at Shawnee Mission, a wealthy suburb in Johnson County, outside Kansas City, Hogue ran and won a race, quickly changed, and sat on the rock wall above the track. Keith was sitting below him on the track in his sweats. One of the prettiest of the Shawnee Mission cheerleaders came over and looked up at Hogue. "Didn't you just run? Didn't you just win?" she asked. Hogue answered, "Yes, I did." He looked over at Keith Mark to make sure he had taken in the scene. "See, they notice," he said. He never wore anything that said "Washington High School" on it.

His room at home was equally bare of identifying details. There were no posters or pictures of his family or a girl. There was a clock on the wall, Mark remembered, and he kept his running shoes on the floor and his sweats in a cardboard box under his bed. It was the kind of setup that suggested that the occupant of the room might be gone in a matter of weeks or days, or had never really been there at all.

Hogue's father, Eugene, was a fixture at the races, Mark remembered. He stood by himself and rooted for the Washington High School runners to win. Hogue's parents were quiet and not particularly demonstrative. He used to see them together, a nice older couple, walking around the neighborhood after dinner, not talking much but standing close to each other and often holding hands. What the parents of Wyandotte County wanted for their children was a life that would allow them to spend weekends with their family and then to wake up Monday morning, put on a suit, and drive to the office in a shiny new American-made car. Their children would never have to climb telephone poles in a jumpsuit that said Union Pacific, carry heavy boxes, or stand like prisoners out in the cold.

Jim Hogue was the most interesting person that he had ever known. There are things that he wishes he hadn't done over the course of his eventful life, but the thought of altering them doesn't make sense. It is more like an entire series of actions that he would need to change or alter since the beginning of time. In order to understand why that was so, it was necessary to understand who he was and where he came from—an assertion about the rootedness of the individual personality in which Jim Hogue had no particular interest, although he was sometimes willing to play along.

Growing up in Kansas City, you play with your friends and go to school. His neighborhood was made up of streets of row houses on what most people would consider to be pretty big lots. His next-door neighbor on one side was an airline pilot. The guy on the other side ran the Kansas turnpike. The couple across the street was retired. Most of the people in the neighborhood were blue-collar professionals. His parents fit the neighborhood pretty well. They were way above average in intelligence and about average in education. His father never talked about his work, and he didn't compliment his son very often. Jim liked running because you know exactly where you stand. You know exactly where you placed and how fast you ran. Every race you run is always part success and part failure, whether you win the race or not. You always run faster than your body thinks you can, but you never run as fast as you want to.

The Hogues had irises growing around the house, so Jim and his friends would hide in those, or play in the tree house. He was friends with Keith Mark, and Connie Campbell and Judith Rowley. His mom made special vegetarian meals at Jim's request, like brown rice mixed with yogurt and salsa, salads, and broiled tomatoes. She cooked the other kids whatever they asked for, including hamburgers. Jim became a vegetarian when he was eight or nine years old. He walked into the house one day and said, "Now I'm a vegetarian," and Jim's mom said, "Okay." He had learned about being a vegetarian from a yoga book he had read in the library.

Stealth and deception were as important to becoming a winning runner as they were in real life, Jim told his friend Keith Mark. "Don't be a know-it-all," he used to tell Keith, who hung on his mentor's every word. "You know, you may be the smartest guy in the world. There may be ten things to know on one particular topic, and you may know nine of them, which makes you the world-renowned expert. But if you go around and tell everybody all nine things you know then you're not the only guy who knows those things, and you're not the smartest guy in the world anymore." It was important to keep your mouth shut, and to listen to what other people had to say. "Even though you know nine things, and no one else knows what you know," he instructed, "if the guy you're talking to only knows one thing, and it's the one thing you don't know, then you let him tell you that thing. Then you know ten things."

Mark appreciated his friend's advice. Jim was the best runner he had ever seen, and his powers of concentration were something close to superhuman. Once, Jim pointed out a kid from Leavenworth High School and told Mark to follow that kid until a certain part of the track, where he should start his final kick. It was a cold day, and Keith was jumping up and down to keep limber as he listened to his friend plot out his strategy for the race. "I came down with my long spikes on the back of Jim's Achilles," he remembered. His spikes raked down the back of Hogue's leg and tore through his shoe. "I'm not talking about a little poke," Mark remembered. "It required stitches." As he watched the blood drip down the back of Hogue's leg and onto the heel of his sneaker, Mark worried that he had maimed Washington High's best runner, possibly for life. "Now, I want you to make your kick here," Hogue continued, without missing a beat. Then he lined up and ran the race.

Hogue was intent on training Keith Mark to steal glory from their teammate Dan Ford, a talented runner who did everything by the book. Hogue hated Dan Ford's guts. If Jim was going to run twelve quarter miles, he'd tell Dan he was going to run two easy miles and call it a day. He wasn't interested in making the team better. He was interested in making a few people better, in part as a way of showing up coach Wayne Hobelman, a painfully modest man who had come to Washington High School to coach football and wound up coaching track. Hogue refused to share any credit with Hobelman. For his part, Hobelman found it hard to understand what made his star runner tick. Hogue refused to run cross-country for Hobelman his junior year, and only ran his senior year in order to get into college. He insisted on doing his own workouts. Under pressure from the school principal, Hobart Neill, who wanted the team to win the state championship, Hobelman asked the team to vote on whether Jim could work out on his own and stay on the team. The team agreed that having Jim run made the team better.

At one point that year, Hobelman called in Jim's parents to talk about their son. His mother seemed shy, the old track coach remembered. She was soft-spoken and apologetic, and said, "I'm sorry for the way Jim acts sometimes." Gene Hogue took his son's side. "Here's a kid that has really worked hard to get where he is. He's worked much harder than the rest of them," he told Hobelman.

Hogue was a discipline problem, but he was also the craftiest runner that Hobelman ever coached. He became the state champion in the two-mile race in his junior year. When Hobelman tried to enter him in the two-mile again the next year, Hogue refused. "He kind of sneered at me," Hobelman remembered. "But I stayed with it. That was one battle I won with Jim."

Twenty years later, Hobelman would still vividly remember the race that Jim ran on a windy day in Wichita for the state championship. Jim was a skinny kid, and the wind was so bad that it nearly blew him off the track. For five or six laps, he stayed even with his main challenger, a fast kid from Wichita West. With two laps to go, the wind picked up even harder, and Hogue started sprinting with the wind at his back. His coach didn't understand why. "Jim, what are you doing!" Hobelman yelled. He tried to catch Hogue's attention, to signal that he still had two laps to go. Hogue ignored him, and began his final kick well before the end of the race. After sprinting thirty yards ahead of the pack, he settled back into his pace, as the runners rounded the curve into the wind.

"I've never seen anybody do that again," Hobelman remembered, shaking his head at his memory of the runner who outsmarted everyone on the track, including his coach. "He wasn't just out there running. He was thinking, and had a plan." As Hogue disappeared into the stands, his coach ran after his new state champion. "I wanted to give him a hug. He went to his parents, I think, and was talking to them. I said, 'Hey, Jim, congratulations.' He tried to stay away from me." Hogue didn't want his coach to get any of the credit. He ran his own race and won.

It was natural that Kansas State, the traditional track powerhouse, recruited Hogue aggressively, but the school backed off when Hobelman described Hogue as a talented runner but also a discipline problem. Still, dozens of schools were interested in Hogue, who chose the University of Wyoming, up in the mountains where he and Keith Mark had always dreamed of living.

In September 1977, James Hogue entered the University of Wyoming, where the competition was even fiercer than it had been in Kansas. Hogue's passionate sense of determination is evident in nearly every line of the detailed letters of instruction that he mailed back home to Keith Mark:

> . . . the higher up that you start, the safer your position will be. The first impressions you give the other runners could be very important in whether you make the team or not. Let them know very little about yourself.
> . . . You should wear either a plain T-shirt or that Wyoming shirt, but remember the less they know about you the better.
> Sunday P.M. Go for an enjoyable but difficult run today of about ten miles. You may run with someone

else today. For the last mile of the run, try to be under
five minutes. Sprints. Then more sprints. Then 5 more.
From your house: Go to 8th and State then South to
Riverview. West on Riverview till it stops. Go left till
Kansas Avenue. West on Kansas till it ends. Turn right
and go to Riverview. West on Riverview to 110th. You
may get water at the Baptist Church. There is a faucet
on the outside of the building. Go North on 110 to
State. Turn right and go home. Lift weights. . . . Go to
Victory hills and run on the South fairway. You may
take your shoes off. Run from the two corner greens
charging up the hill each time.

The solitary intensity of these letters also has something to do
with the particular circumstances in which James Hogue found
himself as a freshman at the University of Wyoming in Laramie.
The coach of the university's track team, Ron Richardson, was a
former assistant at East Tennessee State University who arrived
in Laramie in the fall of 1977 with the dream of turning
Wyoming into a running powerhouse that would rival the University of Texas at El Paso program run by Ted Banks, and the
legendary University of Oregon program run by Bill Bowerman,
which produced the great American Olympic champion Steve
Prefontaine. The class of track-and-field athletes that Richardson
had recruited that year was among the strongest in the country.
In addition to James Hogue, it included Ron Wartgow, a four-
minute miler from Deerfield, Illinois; Jared Thenley, a six-foot-
seven, 260-pound discus thrower from Kansas; and Mike White,
a champion high jumper from inner-city Philadelphia.

The members of his team that year remembered Richardson
as a cold, distant figure who lived and breathed the sport of
running, and who met with his athletes underneath the bleachers
of the university's indoor track in a small, cramped office deco-

rated with a dog-eared copy of *The Management Techniques of Genghis Khan*. As the skies grew dark and temperatures plunged below freezing, Richardson would push his runners through thirty-two 220-meter sprints, followed by sixteen quarter miles and eight half-mile runs. Having read that sprinters would retain the muscle memory of running times faster than those of which they were ordinarily capable, he also evolved a unique training system for his distance runners. Wrapping a weightlifter's belt around the runner's waist, he would attach the belt to a rope approximately eight to ten feet in length. He would then tie the rope around his hand, with a towel underneath to guard against rope burns, and tow the runner up and down the high-altitude mountain trails around Laramie with his arm hanging out of the driver's side window of his Volkswagen Bug. When his runners lost a race at Brigham Young University, he drove them home that night and then picked them up early the next morning, dropped them off seventeen miles from Laramie, and told them to run home.

The true stars of Richardson's recruiting class did not arrive on campus until later that fall. The rules then governing athletic recruitment at American universities did not place limits on the origins or age of athletes, or mandate a capacity to do college-level work. And when Richardson's high school athletes took the track for their first meet that fall, they were joined by their coach's secret weapon, a collection of world-class runners from Kenya, including the future Olympians Michael Chrono, Simon Killerly, and Joseph Nzau. The Kenyans were cagey about their ages. Most were in their mid to late twenties, the age at which runners reach the peak of their mental and physical development. Older and stronger, the Kenyans quickly established their dominance over American athletes who were straight out of high school.

More than two decades later, the American runners at the

University of Wyoming would still remember the experience of being thrown into annihilating daily competition with the world-class runners from Kenya. "People . . . were struggling in their own way with the acclimation to a college program with a very demanding coach . . . in a peer group that was very challenging, even at this level of very high-caliber American athletes," remembered Mike Penny, then a freshman from Colorado. "All of a sudden, there's . . . these foreign athletes, who are so far beyond, not even close to where [we] were at that time." If Richardson's strategy placed a great psychological burden on the American runners, it did pay off on the track. By the spring of 1977, the University of Wyoming team, led by the Kenyans, was ranked third in the country behind Oregon and El Paso.

Penny would later become close friends with the Kenyan runner Joseph Nzau. In the fall and spring of 1977, however, he spent more time with Hogue, who wore a jacket and tie to classes on a campus where most students favored T-shirts and jeans. His elliptical style of communication appeared to be an attempt to copy the Kenyans, who spoke in metaphors and avoided answering direct questions, especially about their true ages. "You'd ask them something like, 'Hey, Joseph, how old are you?' " Penny remembered. "And he'd say, 'Why does it matter how old I am? A tree is old, does it matter how old the tree is?' "

Having been warned by Richardson not to reveal their ages, the Kenyans had reason to be canny. Hogue was the only one of the American high school runners who refused to concede superiority to the older, stronger Kenyans. Instead, Hogue pushed himself to the limits of his physical endurance and beyond in order to compete with runners who were more physically mature and, to Penny's eye at least, more gifted. Hogue ran with the Kenyans. He ran on his own in the mountains. He copied Joseph Nzau's training methods, which included running on the freeways outside Laramie while wearing heavy construction boots in two feet of snow. Soon, Hogue's body began to break down under the stress of a training regimen that was far more demanding than anything he had imposed on Keith Mark. Injured, he ran on the indoor track whose soft dirt surface was less likely to aggravate pulled muscles and damaged tendons. He ran in the swimming pool. He searched the running literature for new training methods that might help him improve his times.

"The symptoms of the beginning of staleness are the opposite of the symptoms of successful sharpening; the runner no longer wishes to race," he wrote to Mark that spring. "His resistance to colds and other infections is lower, and he likely is suffering from tendon and muscle soreness. Finally, there is a pronounced decline in will."

The impressive if uneven results of this regimen are apparent in a letter Hogue sent to his friend at the end of May:

"I got your letter just before my last test. I've studied 37 hours for this one," Hogue wrote.

These past two weeks have been really exhausting. . . .
Indoors. Air Force anchor mile relay 51.6 2nd
Colo State 1000 1st 2m relay 1:58.9 2nd
Colorado 300 way back 32.71 mile 2nd 4:16.38 . . .
Outdoors. Colo State 800 8th 1:52.84 57.0 . . .
Oregon 800 2nd 1:51.61 50.3
I actually don't remember the last 220, and was unconscious for ten minutes afterwards . . . I could have run the 1500 and 800 at WAC, but I didn't especially want to get clobbered, so the coach put me in a marathon that week. They got 21 inches of snow the day before . . . But I ran anyway, mainly because the roads were closed and [I] couldn't get back.

"Try to come out here," he urged his friend, before signing off, "Indubitably in Big Wyoming, Jim."

XI. The Storm

That summer, Hogue found a job with a professor at the University of Wyoming, which gave him backcountry passes to restricted areas of the Rocky Mountain National Park. When Keith Mark came to visit, the two friends immediately set off into the mountains with their passes, sleeping bags, and backpacks for what promised to be an extraordinary outdoor adventure. Hogue's job was collecting butterflies, and when the two friends stopped to camp at night they would lay out a sheet and hook a black light up to the motorcycle battery. The moths would come, and Hogue would put them in a jar of formaldehyde, then pin their wings as if they were in flight. For the two friends from Kansas City, the mountains had always symbolized a kind of solitary freedom, the absence of the limits they associated with their hometown. Later, Keith Mark would date the change in his friend to the last day of that trip, when the two climbers were caught at the top of a mountain by a fierce summer storm.

"It's that time in the mountains where it's summer and it's sunny," he remembered. "And over the top of the peaks comes some black clouds and a strong wind. And the temperature dropped. And I was quite a bit higher in elevation than he was at the time. You know, we were probably half a mile apart. Then all of a sudden, lightning started just zinging by. And Jim was yelling, 'You gotta get down!' You know, I had my pack with a metal frame. And he was yelling, 'Get down! You gotta get down!' "

As lightning struck the peak, they burrowed into the exposed side of the mountain, which was wet and slippery and beginning to freeze over. Sliding down the side of the mountain in a blizzard of ice, Mark made his way to where his friend had stopped. As the lightning struck around them, they got up and ran for the safety of the tree line. "You could feel the ice pelting you, you know?" he remembered. "And the lightning was fierce. You could just hear it. It was like running a key down a wire. Makes the hair stand up on your arms, you know? It was the daytime, but you would see the flash and the thunder would just be there. It was unbelievable. And we just sat there. Nobody said anything. We're soaked to the bone. Scared. Cold."

Hogue didn't say a word when the lightning struck. He didn't speak when the lightning struck a few yards from his head. He didn't speak when the hail stopped, and it started to snow, and the two friends, shivering, in shorts, made their way down the mountain to find that the park had been closed. He didn't speak as they walked along the road in the hopes that someone would be out driving in the storm and would pick them up before they were stricken with exposure. A truck finally picked them up and drove them out of the park to a convenience store, where they changed their clothes and bought chocolate milk and donuts.

The friend Mark knew was never scared. He trained alone, so that no one would see him throw up at the end of a punishing run and interpret his exhaustion as weakness. After that day on the mountain, Mark said, Hogue seemed less sure of himself. "There's no doubt in my mind that what turned Jim's world around is what happened that day in Colorado," Mark insisted, many years later. "Maybe he realized that he was a mortal just like everyone else." When Mark visited his friend in Wyoming the next summer, he found car stereos stacked up in one of the rooms. There were bicycles that Hogue didn't own. The bicycles and the stereos suggested that he was trafficking in stolen goods.

That same summer, Hogue came over to Mark's house in Kansas City. When he left, Mark noticed that he was missing a gold medal he had won in the Kansas Relays—one major high school event that Hogue had never won. When he called his friend to ask about the medal, Hogue denied that he had it. A day later, Hogue called back to say that his mother had found the medal on his driveway. Their friendship was over.

Because Mark knew Hogue so well, it is only fair to admit the possibility that his friend recognized the fact of his own mortality in a single, devastating moment on an exposed mountain peak filled with thunder, hail, and lightning. Given Hogue's reaction to the lightning storm in the mountains with Jon Luff, it is possible that the incident disturbed him in some deeper way. Perhaps it was symbolic of his failure to transcend the limits of his body through training and willpower alone. Perhaps Hogue lost confidence after failing to compete against the superior Kenyan runners. In 1984, Hogue's former teammate Joseph Nzau, representing Kenya, had broken quickly out in front of the pack during the finals of the marathon in the Los Angeles Olympics and held the lead for more than twenty miles before fading just at the end of the race. "Undoubtedly, James Hogue saw this on TV," wrote Mike Penny, in one of the several e-mails he sent me after our interview. "[D]id seeing Nzau on the worldwide stage of the Olympics rekindle thoughts of greatness that led to his enrollment at Palo Alto—just months later? Maybe. An interesting coincidence, at least."

The record of James Hogue's life is marked by blank spaces, and by a series of deliberate distortions and erasures. It contains no shortage of possible reasons why its author might wish to start his life over, and become someone new. It is possible that by coming back to college in the role of older Kenyans he was trying to erase the hurt of having to complete against the more mature athletes. If so, it is interesting that his repeated injuries, most of which were purely imaginary, protected the younger runners on the Princeton team from suffering the same humiliation that had he suffered at their age. If the causes of Hogue's disturbance lay in his family history, those causes were not apparent to Penny, who met Hogue and his father for lunch one afternoon in Lawrence at the Kansas Relays. Eugene Hogue, he recalled, "seemed like a distinguished, very normal, man."

In 1979, Hogue dropped out of Wyoming and moved to Texas, attending a community college and then the University of Texas at Austin, where he studied chemical engineering; he stopped taking classes just a few credits shy of gaining a degree. He was arrested on a charge of theft from a bicycle store in Austin. He was living an experience which is at once more particular and also more universal, of losing confidence, drifting through one's early and mid-twenties, and waking up in a storage shed in Utah one morning and deciding to become someone new.

XII. The Confidence Man

James Hogue phoned me for the first time three days after I returned from Aspen. He said that he was impressed by the research that had gone into the videotape and the letter, and that he would be happy to meet in New York. When he arrived, a few weeks later, his manner was bashful. He looked down at the ground. His face was youthful but weathered, and he wore a baseball cap over his thinning brown hair. He answered my questions in a way that avoided rudeness while limiting the amount of information he revealed. His expression remained mild and impassive, in a way that made me think of the even fluorescent light in an office building whose occupants have all gone home for the night.

Getting into Princeton was like a game, he said. The part he liked best was researching the character and writing the application. He had taken the SAT himself. He could have scored higher, except didn't finish one of the math sections on purpose.

"Why didn't you want a perfect score?" I asked him.

"Only a few people get perfect scores," he told me. A perfect score would have drawn unwanted attention before the application process began.

I asked him what the experience of being at Princeton under an assumed identity had felt like. "Let's imagine that I was creating you as a character on paper," I said, after he'd dodged the question a number of times. "What did you love? What made you uncomfortable? What made you happy? What did you do when you were just feeling quiet? What did your actions mean to you?"

He was silent. "Well, I had a flicker of an idea and then I forgot it," he finally replied. He had promised not to answer questions

about the people he knew at Princeton, he told me. One month
after our meeting in New York, he made another trip east and we
drove down to Princeton. It was funny to be back on campus, he
said. He got up the next morning and ran ten miles. Then we
went to his old dormitory room, 141 Holder Hall.
"It was a nice little room," he remembered. "A fireplace, two
little bedrooms, a little living room. It was all oak-paneled and
had wood floors. This is Holder courtyard," he said, gesturing out
to the expanse of lawn in front of us. "They have five billion dollars and they still can't grow grass here."
The story Hogue told me corresponded in most of its particu-
lars with the story I had heard before. He was born in Wyandotte
County, Kansas. He liked to run. He had read *The Great Gatsby*
in high school and was a fan of Geoffrey Wolff's *The Duke of Deception*, a memoir about the author's father, an inveterate liar and
con artist.
In his own account, James Hogue was an average person, the
youngest of four children. His parents were rural people who had
grown up out West. The names of his sisters were Theresa, Vicki,
and Betty. His father, Eugene, routed boxcars on the Union Pacific railroad. The Kansas City neighborhood where they lived
was a safe environment, he said, with streets of row houses with
flower gardens in the backyards and trees to sit under during the
summer. No one in the neighborhood did anything out of the ordinary. "If I was ten years old and it was the summer," he remembered, "I would have probably been out in the yard playing. We
had irises growing, so we'd hide in those or play in the tree house
or go down to the woods. It was usually pretty hot, so you don't really want to roll around in the grass or anything, with the chiggers
and things like that. I really don't remember too much about it."
In junior high school, he said, he was the best runner in Wyandotte County. He learned to visualize himself winning races. He
learned that there is a time in which you are capable of running

the race that remains true no matter who you are or where you are in the world. His father came to all of his races, he remembered. "What was he like?" I wondered. "Quiet," he answered. "Really terse." "Did he compliment you on winning?" "I can't really remember that. I mean, there weren't any compliments to be given. I was winning all the races." He didn't remember his father being either happy or sad. He said he barely remembered the night on the mountain that had so impressed Keith Mark; it was "maybe a little hairy," but it did not affect him in any important way. He never expected to be able to beat the Kenyans he ran with in college; they were Olympic-caliber athletes. "When you're running against somebody who's been in the Olympics and you're sixteen years old," he said, exaggerating his relative youth by a year, "you don't expect to beat them. It's not a disappointment to you if you don't beat them." He would never reach their level as a runner.

"I just didn't have the genetic ability," he said. "They were superior, really superior athletes," he added. "You're talking about a one-in-a-billion person. I never thought I would be that good." After the death of a grandmother who lived in Wyoming, he left Laramie and moved to Austin. He stopped taking classes when he ran out of money. He felt it was wrong to ask his parents for money, he said. He worked in a lab and built houses.

I noticed at a certain point that he seemed to have a definite aversion to saying the name "Alexi Santana," so I asked him why. "I'm just not used to talking about myself in the third person," he answered. "I'm not a football player or a boxer or something." I thought that was an interesting answer.

"So when you say 'myself,' you include Alexi Santana," I asked him.

"Yeah."

There were other questions I wanted to answer:

Q: What have you been thinking about for the last ten
years? What interests you about what you did here?
A: I don't know. I mean, the things that interested me are
the abstract things. The specific things I think are boring.
Q: Abstract things? Like what?
A: Why did I do this? Why did that work? Why didn't that
work?
Q: Why did you do it? Why didn't it work?
A: Because they found out it was all a fraud.

The questions I was asking him weren't real questions, he explained. They were the products of a story line in my head, whose
relation to his life was at best coincidental.

The day that Jim Hogue first arrived in Princeton it was raining,
he said. He had been living in Las Vegas, building houses during
the day and hanging out at the casinos at night. When I asked
him whether he won much, he shrugged. "You never win," he
said. His friends in Las Vegas had helped him create the character of Santana. They drove him to the airport, and some people
from Princeton picked him up in a car. Being at Princeton was
like being an actor in a play.

He remembered the rain. He had been living out in the
desert, he said, and he hadn't seen rain for a very long time.
Princeton wasn't as intellectually rarefied as some might imagine, he added. "They certainly weren't talking about Plato," he
remembered. "I don't think anybody at this school does that."
People seemed unaware that they were rich. He remembered
having lunch one day with a girl he didn't know well. "She would
be describing her house," he recalled, "and say it has five bed-

rooms, and they have five cars or something, and I'm, like, 'Wow! You're rich!' And she goes, 'Oh, no. Not at all. You know, we're poor.' " He didn't understand how someone like that could go through life thinking she was poor.

"Are these the details that you wanted?" he asked. He admired Peter Hessler, who ran track, and who went to the library most nights and took reams of notes on the books he read. Hessler came from a town in Missouri, Hogue recalled, and he liked to shoot water balloons across the quad with launchers made out of surgical tubing. So it was hard to say that the people he met at Princeton were alike in any particular way.

"How would the world be different if people were allowed to make up any story they wanted?" I asked him.

"They are allowed to do that," he said. "Somebody invented whatever name you got. And up to a certain point in life, that's all you have. And then you start obtaining your own things. So I guess I see it more as an evolution within the self," he added. "And I think it occurs in everybody."

He began to drift and then he kept drifting from one thing to another, playing little games that occupied his mind. He liked pushing other people's buttons. He said that playing with other people's heads made him uncomfortable, but the truth was, he liked it. He liked imagining what he wanted to accomplish and then making it real. When the people he befriended found out that he was actually a different person, with a different life story, they could be freaked out, angry, hurt. But the truth is that we live in a society where people are inventing themselves all the time. The first impostor he ever heard of was a kid down in Wichita who had a friend in the high school registrar's office.

"You said you personally know fifteen people who have done this successfully in similar situations," I asked him.

"At least," he answered. They wrote him letters, he said.

He admitted that what he had done belonged, perhaps, to a different category of invention. "I was just using the basic fact that people are going to believe whatever they're told unless they have a good reason not to," he said. What made his actions possible, he explained, was his ability to tolerate guilt. His habit of wearing a mask was simply an impulse that he couldn't control. "Say you're a diabetic," he explained. "You know you can't eat certain foods, but you do it anyway."

What really interested him was the process of psychological manipulation that helped him to fill in the blanks in the appropriate way that would generate the result that he wanted. "The character itself was just something I made up," he explained. The finer points of Santana's biography were arrived at by trial and error. "It was the process of trying to figure out what would push other people's buttons, I guess. You know, it's a harsh thing to do, but. . . ." He didn't feel guilty about lying at all.

We had been together at Princeton now for three days straight, and there were still many questions that I wished to ask, and that I hoped he might answer. Being around rich people had its upsides and its downsides, he said. "The only reason I would rather be near them is because what I do for a living sort of requires being around them," he told me. "In fact, I'd rather not be around them. I'd rather not be around anybody, to tell you the truth."

"What are you doing now?" I asked him.

"I'm building a house," he told me.

XIII. The Freshman

The story of Alexi Santana was a way of redeeming the injuries
James Hogue had experienced in his life, or so I imagined. The
eighteen-year-old runner whose spirit had been broken came
back ten years later to reclaim what had been taken from him,
only to be broken again, by something that was larger and more
powerful than he was. Some parts of his stories were verifiable.
Others were not. I knew at least that I could trust him on one
count: the story of his life would have only a tangential relation to
whatever version of it I chose to write. The act by which America
transformed itself into a supernova of self-invention—a stupe-
fying explosion of individuals guaranteed the right to pursue
their own happiness—meant that in every generation Americans
would break free from the past and make themselves over. Living suspended between the present and the future, 300 million
flowers bloom in midair.

"I think it's a common fantasy," Jim told me, when I asked him
whether making yourself up from scratch as an entirely new person is really possible, even in America. "What I know about it is
that you can do it in actual fact if you really want to. And you can
probably only do it so long, before you have to go back to where
you started out."

That the dream of becoming someone new is doomed to failure is not really so bad, since every story ends in failure. It's just a
particular kind of story, that's all.

"How did your parents feel when this thing hit the papers?" I
asked Jim once.

"Well, they didn't have any questions about it that they asked
me," he said, in his diffident way, looking down at the floor of his

old dorm room at Princeton. "But yeah, they were embarrassed and perplexed."

At one point during my last conversation with Hogue at Princeton, a freshman named Dennis Dugan entered Hogue's old room, which was his room now, to retrieve his coat. "It seems like everyone is a Princeton alumnus," the freshman said. "That's what some people are saying." He was friendly and open-faced. He was eager to meet the man who had lived in his room however many years ago. Hogue was eager to talk to him, too. He was glad to play the role of a Princeton alumnus, offering avuncular advice about the eating clubs and the food. When I think about James Hogue, I find it hard not to return to that day, which was the only time I ever saw him look truly happy and at ease.

"A lot of people tend to put the little stickers on their cars," Hogue told the freshman. "So, I mean, you'll see that and you'll probably stop and talk to them. There's one fellow in Aspen. Oh, he must be sixty or seventy. He's got an orange car, bright orange, with the tiger on the little antenna and stickers in the windows. I mean, you'll see stuff like that. And you'll probably go to work on Wall Street and I'm sure you'll run into people there." I sat on the fold-out couch and took notes.

"They say college is the best time of your life," Dugan said. "Do you believe that?"

"I think it's supposed to be," Hogue responded.

"What are some of your memories, Jim?" I asked.

"He's living them," Hogue answered. "He'll remember." He turned to Dugan. "I mean, have you had your nude Olympics yet?"

The freshman appeared eager to keep the moment alive, to maintain this fleeting connection to a person who had gone this way before. "I think he has great memories of this place," he offered, as Hogue stood by with a mild, quizzical expression on his face. "I think he had a lot of fun here. I think it really helped him out. Not just the diploma itself but the actual things that he learned while obtaining that diploma . . . not just the actual facts and figures and theory, just the existence, how to exist with people. I know a lot of people, they've had their own room their whole life." I thought about the storage shed in Utah with the bare light bulb and the aluminum walls. I thought about the stolen bicycles. I thought about what Princeton had meant to Hogue. I saw that he was smiling.

"I don't want special preference just because of the name of my club," the freshman was saying. "I want to prove myself."

"But you'll put that on your résumé," Hogue said. There was nothing bitter in his voice, I realized.

Dugan had worked hard to get to Princeton, he said. He had grown up in New Jersey in a middle-class family, just above the line that allows you to raise your head to see the path before you and win a scholarship to prep school. The day he found out he was accepted at Princeton was the best day of his life. "For the week after that, I was sort of in disbelief," he went on.

"So you would tell all your friends to work hard and to do—"

"Yeah. I tell my little brother every day," Dugan said.

"How old is he?" Hogue asked.

"He's eight."

"Because," Hogue said, "they really like to let in brothers and sisters and friends."

The freshman nodded. He liked that idea. He would grow older, protected by the circle of shared experience and tradition that binds Princetonians together, secure in the benefits of a good education and a wealth of useful contacts that would ease his way through the snares and thickets of life. Being accepted at Princeton was a blessing, he said. Everything he had seen about the place was exactly as it was described in the brochures.